Sartre

OTHER TITLES IN THE ONEWORLD PHILOSOPHERS SERIES

Descartes, Harry M. Bracken, ISBN 1–85168–294–5
Hobbes, Eugene Heath, ISBN 1–85168–292–9
Nietzsche, Robert Wicks, ISBN 1–85168–291–0
Wittgenstein, Avrum Stroll, ISBN 1–85168–293–7

Sartre

Neil Levy

ONEWORLD PHILOSOPHERS

ONEWORLD

OXFORD

SARTRE

Oneworld Publications
(Sales and Editorial)
185 Banbury Road
Oxford OX2 7AR
England
www.oneworld-publications.com

ISBN 1–85168–290–2

Cover design by the Bridgewater Book Company
Cover image © Hulton Deutsch Collection/CORBIS
Typeset by Saxon Graphics Ltd, Derby, UK
Printed and bound by Clays Ltd, St Ives plc

Contents

Preface

When Sartre died in 1980, more than fifty thousand people watched the slow procession of his coffin through the streets of Paris. An extraordinary scene: very rarely in the history of Western thought has a mere philosopher commanded such respect from his contemporaries. Moreover, Sartre's fame extended well beyond France. The news of his death made the front pages of not only the major French newspapers like *Le Monde* (which devoted a full eight pages to his passing) and *Le Figaro*, but also the *New York Times* and the *Washington Post*. The then president of Italy sent a message of condolence to Simone de Beauvoir, Sartre's closest companion, and Valéry Giscard d'Estaing, the then president of France went to the hospital where Sartre had died and sat in a solitary vigil for a full hour.

How did it come about that the death of a man who occupied no official positions, had never been elected to any body nor even held a university post could prompt such an extraordinary outpouring of adulation and respect from across the world? France has traditionally been a country that honours its intellectuals – when Michel Foucault died four years later, the news once again made the front pages of the French press – but even by French standards the reaction was extraordinary. How does a mere philosopher become so prestigious, and so renowned?

In fact, Sartre was not *just* a philosopher. Far from it; there were few literary genres to which he did not turn his hand. He published his first novel, *Nausea*, in 1938, to critical acclaim. It was to be followed by three others in the 1940s. In the interim, Sartre had turned to the stage. His first play was performed in the prisoner-of-war camp in which he was detained following the German occupation of France; subsequently he would become a prolific playwright. He also wrote short stories, biographies of French literary greats (including a massive – and unfinished – study of Flaubert, which runs to well over two thousand pages), an autobiography, political commentary, aesthetic criticism. Sartre was above all a writer. In 1964 he was offered, and declined, the Nobel Prize for literature: Sartre's fame as an author was international.

Though his literary output goes some way to explaining his celebrity, Sartre was perhaps even better known as a political activist than as a writer. The Sartre who penned *Nausea* was rather apolitical: beyond a contempt for those who unthinkingly follow the dictates of convention, he advocated no causes. But the experience of the Second World War shook him out of his apathy. During the war, he contributed in a small way to the Resistance; after it, he wrote and spoke widely in favour of socialism and against the policies of the French right. Together with a few like-minded thinkers, he founded his own intellectual review, *Les Temps Modernes* (*Modern Times*) – still a major presence on the French intellectual scene – in part to further discussion of his political views.

As the years passed, Sartre became more outspoken, and more radical. He supported the Algerians in their struggle for independence from France, and was branded a traitor by many for so doing. He signed an illegal petition denouncing the behaviour of the French military in Algeria. He faced arrest over the petition until General Charles de Gaulle, president of France, announced that no action would be taken against him. 'You do not imprison Voltaire,' de Gaulle is reported as saying. Even if no official measures were taken against him, Sartre did not escape completely unscathed. His apartment was bombed twice by far-right terrorists, and the offices of *Les Temps Modernes* were also attacked. 'Shoot Jean Paul Sartre,' demonstrators chanted in the street.

Sartre would remain a political activist as long as his health held out. His voice was to be heard everywhere – denouncing American involvement in Vietnam (he participated in the tribunal organized by Bertrand Russell, the only Anglophone philosopher whose prestige approached that of Sartre, which found the US and its allies guilty of war crimes in Vietnam), protesting against racism and oppression, assisting the French far-left. As an activist, Sartre was a headline maker. There are some people who claim that it was this very public life which, more than anything else, accounts for Sartre's renown; that it was a life emblematic of a century of French intellectual and political life which the crowd came to salute in 1980. No doubt, there is a great deal of truth in this claim. But it does not fully account for Sartre's influence. To see that this is so, we need only to be reminded that Sartre's fame *preceded* his political involvement, and even his literary renown. It is as a philosopher that Sartre first becomes a major public figure.

Somehow, despite his resistance activities and his literary output, Sartre managed to find the time to write a substantial work of original philosophy during the Second World War. That work, translated as *Being and Nothingness*, was published in 1943 in occupied France. At first it was barely noticed, but by the end of the war it had begun to attract considerable attention from the philosophical community. Nevertheless, Sartre's sudden leap to prominence came as something of a surprise. If we were to attempt to date Sartre's rise precisely, we could do worse than settle on 29 October 1945, the date on which Sartre gave a lecture entitled 'Existentialism is a Humanism'. The organizers of the lecture expected a small, polite audience. They got a near riot, as hundreds of people tried to crowd into a room that would not hold them all. Sartre was suddenly a major force on the Parisian intellectual scene.

Sartre's grip on the popular imagination over the next decade can only be compared to that of the most successful pop stars. It was not only austere philosophers who read and discussed his works. French students, young people generally, took them up enthusiastically. Here was a philosophy that not only sought for intellectual truths; it aimed to transform lives. It called upon each of us to live authentically; that is, to live in accordance with values that we freely and autonomously endorse, rather than those which are merely conventional. It denounced conformism, and in its place offered a thorough-going philosophy of freedom. Moreover, this was a philosophy accessible to anyone with a reasonable level of education, not just to philosophy specialists. If you were such a specialist, *Being and Nothingness* held enough treasures to keep you occupied for decades, but if your philosophical education was limited to a year at high school (in France, philosophy has long been offered in the final year or two of schooling), 'Existentialism is a Humanism' would be challenging enough for you. If you lacked even that degree of training, you could nevertheless read the novels and attend the plays in which Sartre's thought found literary expression.

After the stifling repression imposed upon France by the war, this philosophy came as a breath of fresh air to a whole generation. Soon 'existentialism', as it became known, had a life independent of its best-known exponent. When the cellars of fashionable Saint-Germain-des-Prés were converted into nightclubs, the press dubbed them *caves existentialistes*. Existentialism became synonymous with bohemianism: the one providing the philosophical justification for the other. The association was assisted by Sartre's well-known relationship with Simone de Beauvoir, whose 1949 work *The Second Sex* is a major landmark in feminist philosophy. Sartre and de Beauvoir's unconventional alliance – they decided against marriage, at a time when so doing was still scandalous, and pursued a variety of sexual liaisons outside this principal relationship – seemed a living example of existentialist nonconformism, and provided a role model for generations of young people seeking a new form of relationship in which they could preserve their autonomy. From then on, Sartre's fame grew and became international. A few short years later, his influence would touch the youth of the United States and the United Kingdom, though perhaps with not quite the same force as it had had in France, and departments of philosophy – not to mention literature and politics – would devote courses to his thought.

Thus it was above all as a philosopher that Sartre first made his extraordinary impact. And it is as a philosopher that I propose to treat him here. Sartre the philosopher needs rescuing from Sartre the man, the more so since his philosophical reputation took a battering in the 1960s and the 1970s. In these years, a new generation of thinkers came to prominence in France, a generation that claimed (falsely) not to be influenced by the older man. They denounced his thought at every opportunity as they attempted to steal something of his prestige. Claude Lévi-Strauss, the famous French anthropologist devoted the final chapter of his best-known work, *The Savage Mind*, to criticizing Sartre's thought. After that, the floodgates were opened, and the generation influenced by Lévi-Strauss launched ever more ferocious attacks on Sartre. Michel Foucault's 1966 comment, which focused on Sartre's second major philosophical text, is typical:

> *La critique de la raison dialectique* is the magnificent and pathetic effort of a nineteenth-century man to conceive of the twentieth century. In this sense, Sartre is the last Hegelian, and even, I would say, the last Marxist.[1]

The new generation, who called themselves 'structuralists', claimed that Sartre's thought over-emphasized the creative power of human beings and overlooked the extent to which we are all caught within networks of meaning, structures in fact, which shape our lives and determine our thought. Sartre had been right, they held, to announce in that famous lecture that existentialism is a humanism, but no humanism could account for the manner in which language and the other structured systems underlie our actions and our thoughts. The structuralists, and later the post-structuralists, thus proudly declared themselves anti-humanists, and by this gesture claimed to consign Sartre's thought to the dustbin of history.

In fact, none of these thinkers ever took the time to confront existentialism head on. Their claim that structuralism was superior to existentialism was thus without justification: the work that could justify it had never been done. Nevertheless, perhaps because Sartre had dominated the scene for so long and the intellectual public was hungry for new currents of thought, perhaps because too few people had absorbed Sartre's difficult later work whereas the faults of the earlier were by now apparent, it came to be accepted that structuralism had definitively refuted existentialism. Though still a major figure on the French and the international intellectual scene, Sartre's star was on the wane.

Then, in 1968, came the events that simultaneously were Sartre's finest hour and marked the end of his period of ascendancy. In that year, French university campuses were the focus of a number of demonstrations. Heavy-handed police tactics resulted in many injuries, which served merely to radicalize the student leadership. In May, courses at the Sorbonne were suspended; the students took to the streets. Hundreds were injured and more arrested in the ensuing battles with police. Major unions supported the students, and by 20 May nine million workers were on strike. France seemed poised on the brink of revolution.

But the revolution faltered and died. The still-powerful Communist Party, and the communist-affiliated trade unions opposed further involvement with the students; the movement lost momentum and fractured. De Gaulle offered concessions to the workers, and suddenly the moment had passed. Slowly, life returned to normal in Paris.

In some ways the course of the events of May can be seen as Sartre's finest hour. They offered a remarkable confirmation of the theory of group formation and collapse he had developed in *The Critique of Dialectical Reason*; even the emotions experienced by the participants in the events were as Sartre had predicted. Moreover, the student leaders themselves saw in him an ally. He wrote articles in support of their movement, even interviewing Daniel Cohn-Bendit for *Le Nouvel Observateur*. In return, they invited him to speak to them, in an occupied Sorbonne. Thousands flocked to hear him. Though they insisted that their movement was democratic and spontaneous, and accepted no leaders, they looked to Sartre as a source of inspiration and encouragement.

In fact no one influenced the students more than Sartre. Moreover, the fact that the events followed precisely the course predicted in his work on group formation and collapse seemed to confirm his continued political and philosophical relevance, as did his condemnation of communist inaction. Nevertheless, when it became clear that the revolutionary moment had passed, the decline in Sartre's prestige accelerated.

It is not entirely clear why this occurred. An important part of the explanation undoubtedly involves the plummet in the stocks of Marxism more generally in the wake of the events. A Communist Party already weakened by the increasingly difficult to ignore evidence of brutal Soviet repression had once again failed to distinguish itself; it had seemed as effective a counter-revolutionary force as De Gaulle himself. Of course, Sartre's Marxism was independent of, and in opposition to, that of the communists; he, along with a number of other French intellectuals, had long been arguing that the communists distorted Marx's thought. But the feeling was now growing among those disappointed by the failure of the May movement that it was Marxism itself, and not its more or less able interpreters, which was at fault; that Marxism's day was past, its progressive potential exhausted.

In large part, these criticisms came from the same thinkers who had criticized Sartre's philosophy in the name of structuralism. These thinkers now pointed to the allegedly 'totalizing' essence of Marxism – that is, its inherent tendency to explain all events and institutions as the result of a single cause – and argued that this kind of thinking was insensitive to the sheer contingency of history. Worse, they argued, Marxism worked actively to suppress individual difference. It subordinated all political action to the needs of the proletariat, the working class, under the direction of the Communist Party, and thus was ill suited to acting in a political environment in which progressive forces were increasingly fragmented. Since Marxism would subsume all these forces, the so-called 'new social movements' (feminism, the gay movement, green groups, anti-racism activists, and so on), under the banner of a single party, it would drain them of their power.

For decades, Marxism had been perhaps the single most important force on the French intellectual scene. Quite suddenly, its grip was broken, and the French left began to search for new models, to elaborate new theories. The result was two decades of prodigious intellectual fertility, which threw up names and styles of thought which still occupy an important place on the contemporary intellectual scene, not only in France but also in the Anglophone world. Foucault's archaeology, then his Nietzschean-inspired genealogy,

Derrida's deconstruction, the postmodern thought of Lyotard, the work of Deleuze – a dizzying succession of difficult theories.

For those caught up in this new wave of philosophy, it seemed that Sartre had been left behind. His thought was now out of date, 'essentially relegated to the past'.[2] His humanism represented the last gasp of a naïve philosophy, his Marxism something rather more sinister. Worst of all, his influential interpretation of Heidegger, his acknowledged inspiration, had misrepresented the thought of this truly profound thinker. In order to free ourselves from the confines of a humanism that is not adequate to account for language and other structured systems, to elaborate a politics equal to the demands of new and more complex times, we need simultaneously to go beyond Sartre and to return to his sources. In Heidegger's thought, it was increasingly often claimed, we would find the resources we need to forge the new philosophy. Sartre could play no positive role in this process; far from it, his thought represented an obstruction along the path to truth.

We can be forgiven for remaining sceptical about these sweeping claims. Their most influential statements came from thinkers who, however important in their own right, gave little evidence of having read Sartre in depth. As we shall see, some of their criticisms were valid; they pointed to real flaws in Sartre's early thought. But they remained blind to its virtues; worse still, they seemed ignorant (probably wilfully so, given Sartre's renown) of the later work, in which he corrected these deficiencies. Motivated, perhaps, more by the desire to make a name for themselves than by a desire to understand Sartre, they missed the strengths of his work and thereby had to forgo a valuable resource, one that would have allowed them to correct the faults of their own thought. When philosophy is conducted according to the dictates of fashion, it is the search for truth which is the first casualty.

Sartre died, therefore, a 'has been'.[3] But a new century always brings with it a need to look back on and come to terms with the old. Inevitably, this retrospective would include Sartre, whose life was emblematic of the past century – even his detractors concede that. Inevitably, too, the philosophy, and not just the life, would come in for a second reading. Sartre has found new readers, and old ones returned with new eyes. These readers have found in his work much more than they expected, a much more defensible philosophy than they thought. Reading Sartre, really reading him, with a view to understanding him and applying his thought and not merely looking to score points, is once more back on the agenda.

The signs of revival come both from France and from the Anglophone world. Most telling of these signs has been the impact of Bernard-Henri Lévy's recent *Le Siècle de Sartre* (*Sartre's Century*).[4] Lévy has been a trendsetter on the French intellectual scene for over two decades; his devotion of such a long, critical but respectful work to Sartre's thought and his life could not fail to signify the rehabilitation of the existentialist philosopher. Newspapers and magazines devoted numerous pages, first to reviewing Lévy's book, then to special issues timed to coincide with the twentieth anniversary of Sartre's death. *Libération* and *Le Monde* devoted their book pages to Sartre once more; his photograph appeared on the front cover of *Le Nouvel Observateur*. The square outside the café in Paris which Sartre used to frequent with Simone de Beauvoir was renamed the Place Sartre-de-Beauvoir. In the Anglophone world, Richard Attenborough has announced that he will make a film about the relationship between Sartre, de Beauvoir, and Nelson Algren, de Beauvoir's American lover, and Richard Eyre has recently staged an acclaimed production of Sartre's *Les Mains Sales* (*Dirty Hands*) at London's Almeida theatre. In France, it has become commonplace to speak of the *retour de Sartre* (Sartre's return).

I hope that this book will contribute in some small way to this *retour*. It is as a philosopher that Sartre made his initial and his most lasting impact, and it is as a philosopher that I will treat him here. I do so in the belief that his philosophical work deserves the wider audience it is once more reaching, for the best possible reason: because it is an important contribution to the quest for philosophical truth. Though I shall not hesitate to criticize Sartre when I believe him mistaken, very often he is right; moreover, as we shall see, as his thought develops, his errors are less frequent, his overall position more defensible. We are now beginning to see once more what Sartre's generation did not hesitate to affirm: that Sartre is a great philosopher, whose ideas remain vital. Sartre is, once more, our contemporary.

In a book of this length, it will not be possible to consider all, or even all the most important, topics in Sartre's thought. Since I am considering Sartre as a philosopher, I will almost completely ignore his literary output, his journalism, his political writings and criticism. Even so, my treatment of the philosophy will be very partial. The book on which I will focus, *Being and Nothingness*, is a long and dense treatise, and I shall not have space to discuss all of its themes. My selection of topics is not arbitrary, however. I have chosen to follow a theme in Sartre's thought: the nature and exercise of human freedom. This is no mere caprice on my part; Sartre's thought is indisputably centred around this topic, and his evolution as a philosopher is motivated by the need to rethink it.

Thus, I will elaborate Sartre's thought always with a view to understanding it as a philosophy of freedom. Since freedom is so central to his philosophy, approaching it in this way requires me to discuss most of his central concepts, his ontology and his ethics. I believe that coming at his thought from this direction requires us to recapitulate precisely Sartre's own approach, and the gain in understanding him is immense. Moreover, if I am right in thinking that freedom is so central to his thought, then we are justified in considering topics that are not essential to elaborating Sartre's philosophy of freedom, however interesting in their own right, as relatively peripheral. By approaching him in this manner, we understand Sartre as he recommended we ought to understand a human being: by considering him from his own perspective.

This book is intended as an introduction to Sartre, though I hope it can be read with profit by those who know his work well. Accordingly, I have decided not to overburden the text with scholarly references. Instead, at the end of each chapter I will provide a brief guide to further reading: a short list of books that will aid the reader who wishes to investigate a particular topic in greater depth. Sartre is a complex thinker, but I hope that this book will make him accessible to anyone who is prepared to spend some time and effort engaged in his favourite activity: thinking.

Abbreviations

Since I will be citing some of Sartre's works many times, it is convenient to refer to them in the text with an abbreviation followed by a page number.

BN   *Being and Nothingness*, trans. Hazel E. Barnes (London: Routledge, 1993). Originally published as *L'Être et le Néant* (Paris: Éditions Gallimard, 1943).

CDR   *Critique of Dialectical Reason*, trans. Alan Sheridan-Smith (London: Verso, 1991). Originally published as *Critique de la Raison Dialectique* (Paris: Éditions Gallimard, 1960).

SFM   *Search for a Method*, trans. Hazel E. Barnes (New York: Vintage, 1968). Originally published as 'Question de Méthode', as the prefatory essay to the French edition of CDR.

EH   'Existentialism is a Humanism', trans. P. Mairet, in *Existentialism from Dostoevsky to Sartre*, ed. Walter Kaufmann (New York: New American Library, 1975). Originally published as *L'Existentialisme est un humanisme* (Paris: Éditions Nagel, 1948).

FURTHER READING

Biographical information regarding Sartre's life is drawn from what is to date the best biography of him: Annie Cohen-Solal, *Sartre: A Life* (London: Heinemann, 1985). For an overview of Sartre's life and intellectual development in his own words, see *Sartre by Himself*, trans. Richard Seaver (Melbourne: Outback Press, 1978). This is the text of a film directed by Alexandre Astruc.

Claude Lévi-Strauss's attack on Sartre is contained in the last chapter of his *The Savage Mind* (Chicago: University of Chicago Press, 1966). Derrida adds his voice to the criticisms in 'The Ends of Man', in his *Margins of Philosophy*, trans. Alan Bass (Chicago: University of Chicago Press, 1982). Christina Howells has ably defended Sartre against structuralist and post-structuralist criticism in her *Sartre: The Necessity of Freedom* (Cambridge: Cambridge University Press, 1988). I have attempted to add to her arguments in my own *Being up-to-Date: Foucault, Sartre and Postmodernity* (New York: Peter Lang, 2001).

On the relationship between Sartre and Heidegger, see the appendix to David E. Cooper's *Existentialism: A Reconstruction*, 2nd edn (Oxford: Blackwell, 1999).

For those readers interested in delving deeper into the voluminous literature devoted to Sartre, Francois H. Lapointe's *Jean-Paul Sartre and His Critics: An International Bibliography (1938–1980)*, 2nd edn (Bowling Green, OH: Philosophy Documentation Center, Bowling Green State University, 1981) is indispensable. Michel Rybalka and Michel Contat provide a guide to more recent work in their *Sartre: Bibliography 1980–1992* (Paris: CNRS Editions, 1993).

THE EXISTENTIALIST SARTRE

This book is divided into two parts of very unequal size. The first part is devoted to an elaboration and assessment of the philosophy for which Sartre is best known – existentialism. Sartre's existentialism is explicitly a philosophy of freedom; its first and last concern is the vindication of the essential and irreducible liberty of each person, and with drawing the ethical implications of this freedom. All of Sartre's thought hangs from this central thread; his metaphysics, his theory of knowledge, and so on, all are elaborated in order to support his philosophy of freedom. We shall follow Sartre as he develops the superstructure of this philosophy, then trace the ways in which it supports the central pillar of his work, his theory of freedom itself. Finally, we will turn to an assessment of that theory, examining its strengths and probing its weaknesses. In the much shorter second part of the book, we will examine the less well-known Sartre, the Marxist Sartre. We will see how Sartre's turn to Marxism enabled him to repair gaps in his existentialist thought.

chapter one

Sartre and phenomenology

The full title of Sartre's masterpiece, *Being and Nothingness: An Essay on Phenomenological Ontology*, provides us with a convenient way into his thought. Let us examine the last word of the title first. 'Ontology' is a subdiscipline of philosophy. It is that branch of philosophy which deals with the ultimate constituents of reality, with what the universe consists of most fundamentally. For example, modern science holds that the universe consists of atoms and subatomic particles. At the most fundamental level, that is all there really is; everything else we see and encounter – rocks, trees, water, even people – is built up out of this basic matter. Since science holds that there is only one substance out of which everything is built, its ontology is 'monist'.

But the main title of Sartre's book signals that his ontology will be dualist: that is, it will hold that reality is composed of *two* irreducible elements. The world that science studies is (very roughly speaking, as we shall go on to see) the world of 'being'. But 'being' does not exhaust the entirety of reality. In order to grasp it fully, we must also grasp the place that nothingness occupies in it.

We can already glimpse the first puzzle that Sartre's work poses for us. How can *nothingness* be one of the components of reality? Ontology is concerned with everything that is, but nothingness *is not*. It cannot, therefore, be a component of the reality with which ontology is concerned. This supposed tendency to take nothingness for an entity has infuriated analytical philosophers. In fact, their attribution to Sartre of a simple mistake is based on a misunderstanding: Sartre is not committed to holding that nothingness *is*, but instead to the much more plausible thesis that our experience cannot be explained by reference to an ontology that has a place for only the positive features of being.

In what follows, then, I shall be concerned with correcting this misapprehension, by demonstrating the essential place that nothingness has in our actual experience of the world. I will also be concerned with avoiding another common misconception – the idea that Sartre's dualistic ontology is merely an updated version of the dualism of René Descartes, perhaps the single philosopher who did more than any other to set philosophy on the path to modernity. Descartes argued that the universe consisted of thinking things and extended things – humans being both, a thinking mind inhabiting a body that is fundamentally different from it, and Sartre's dualism certainly parallels this ontology. Nevertheless, Sartre's ontology is no mere rehash of the Cartesian system. Instead, it represents a radical rethinking of the relationship between the self and the world.

Before I begin to elaborate this ontology, however, I want to explore further the subtitle of Sartre's work. This ontology will, he announces, be *phenomenological*. What is phenomenology and in what ways is *Being and Nothingness* phenomenological?

It is rather difficult to answer these questions. Phenomenology does not refer to a single thesis, or even to a unified school. Instead, it names a number of overlapping and loosely related approaches to philosophy, all of which stem from the work of the influential German philosopher Edmund Husserl. I shall not enter into the difficult task of describing Husserl's work and the transformations it underwent. Instead, I shall content myself with sketching the manners in which Sartre saw himself as continuing the phenomenological tradition.

Intentionality

One of the theories for which Husserl is best known is that of the intentionality of consciousness. To say that consciousness is intentional is to say that it always points to ('intends') something outside itself. One of Sartre's early essays is devoted to this thesis.[5] It is worth pausing over, since for Sartre this thesis helped establish that the manner of being of things – of what he called the 'in-itself' – is fundamentally different to the manner of being of consciousness.

Sartre begins his discussion of Husserl's idea by contrasting it to a dominant position in the French epistemology (theory of knowledge) of his day. For many French philosophers, to know something was to draw it *into* consciousness, a process whereby the known thing was incorporated into the knowing subject, so that the two ended up of the same substance. 'O digestive philosophy,' Sartre comments sardonically. But, Sartre holds, this ignores the fundamental difference between things and consciousness. It ignores, that is, that things exist outside consciousness, in such a manner that whether, and how, they are does not and cannot depend on us and what we think of them. As Sartre writes in *Being and Nothingness,*

> A table is not in consciousness – not even in the capacity of a representation. A table is in space, beside the window, etc. The existence of the table in fact is a center of opacity for consciousness; it would require an infinite process to inventory the total contents of a thing … The first procedure of a philosophy ought to be to expel things from consciousness and to reestablish its true connection to the world, to know that consciousness is a positional consciousness of the world. (BN, p. xxvii)

The thesis that consciousness is intentional restores to the world its transcendence, the sheer fact that it is essentially different from consciousness.

Moreover, Sartre holds, consciousness must be intentional because there can never be anything at all inside consciousness; consciousness is always and necessarily empty. Rather than the knowing subject incorporating the known object into itself, Sartre holds, almost exactly the opposite takes place: consciousness is outside of itself, with the object it intends. Thus, Sartre holds, Husserl returns the world to us, in all its transcendence and its fundamental indifference to our wishes and plans. At the same time, however, he shows us that nothing can inhabit consciousness – not even ourselves:

> everything is finally outside, even ourselves. Outside, in the world, among others. It is not in some hiding-place that we will discover ourselves: it is on the road, in the town, in the midst of the crowd, a thing among things, a man among men.[6]

Because consciousness is intentional, nothing can enter into it. And a moment's reflection will show that consciousness must be intentional. To see this, we need only to imagine for a moment that consciousness was *not* intentional; that it really was able to incorporate what it knows into itself, as the French epistemologists had suggested. Gradually, as consciousness incorporated more and more known objects into itself, it would cease to be able to reflect what is outside itself properly. Think of a mirror. If a mirror were to bear the traces of all the objects that it has reflected in the past on its surface, it would quickly cease to be useful. It would be so cluttered with the images of past objects that it would be unable to reflect accurately whatever is before it now. In exactly the same way, if consciousness were permanently marked by what it knows, knowledge could not be trusted to reflect accurately what is known. (This is not to deny that the traces of what is known are permanently retained, in the memory. Instead, Sartre is asserting that consciousness and the memory must be held to be distinct if knowledge is to be possible.)

The priority of lived experience over the objective viewpoint

This, then, is one sense in which Sartre is a phenomenologist. Like Husserl, he is committed to the thesis that consciousness is intentional. There is, however, another sense in which Sartre can justifiably call himself a phenomenologist. The early Husserl had been concerned with establishing phenomenology as a science – in fact, as the culmination of all Western science. The later Husserl, however, increasingly turned his attention away from science and towards the *Lebenswelt* ('life-world'), the world as it is experienced and lived. This lived world is now seen as more fundamental than the world of science. If Sartre is rightfully called a phenomenologist, it is principally because he follows Husserl in holding that we live in a world that is, at bottom, human.

Perhaps we can best appreciate the force of the claim that our world is *fundamentally* human by contrasting it to the view it opposes. This is a view that comes to us from modern science, but it has by now so thoroughly penetrated the consciousness of all of us that it is now also the view of common sense. On the scientific view, we ought to draw a precise distinction between the world as we experience it and the world as it *really* is. The world as we experience it, the subjective world, is the world of values – ethical and aesthetic – the world as hostile or hospitable. It is, advocates of this view insist, essentially an illusion.

The purveyors of the scientific viewpoint have persuasive evidence they can cite in favour of their cause. They can point to the undeniable success of the scientific worldview. It wasn't until science made the distinction they hold to be fundamental, between the objective and the subjective worlds, that it could begin to lay the foundations for its spectacular accomplishments. The scientific revolution became possible only when scientists interpreted the physical world as a system of interlocking causes and effects operating according to its own laws, without reference to our hopes and our values. In contrast, the attempt to view the world as meaningful only held back scientific progress. Think, in this regard, of the debate between Galileo and the Catholic Church over the Copernican system (the question whether the earth revolves around the sun, or vice versa). Galileo was able to produce evidence against the view that the sun revolves around the earth. But the church rejected this evidence *a priori*: the earth *must* be at the centre of the universe, its theologians reasoned, because the Bible (as they interpreted it) said so. We have here, defenders of the scientific viewpoint claim, a paradigm case of the clash between proponents of objective and subjective viewpoints, and a decisive vindication of the former. The church insisted upon seeing the universe as meaningful, and therefore was unable to distinguish what was *really* there from what was mere projection. The scientist, however, suspended his involvement in the world, in order to focus on it as an objective and independent reality. He was thereby enabled to understand it.

Now, whether or not this is an accurate depiction of the conflict between Galileo and the Catholic Church, there does seem to be more than a little validity to the claim here being made. It indeed seems to be the case that understanding the universe as a meaning-less system of causal processes is the precondition of scientific progress. But Sartre is not committed to denying that this is the case. Instead, he wants to attack two related tendencies. First, he wants to point to the pernicious consequences of the over-extension of this kind of thinking, its application in areas in which it is not appropriate. Second, and more fundamentally, he wants to deny the claim that this scientific way of understanding the world is the more basic, the kind of understanding upon which all others are (or should be) parasitic. The truth, Sartre will claim, is exactly the reverse. The scientific mode of understanding the universe is in fact derived from the world as it is experienced in everyday life.

Let us continue to sketch the scientific view, in order to see how it is that it comes to be extended beyond the domain in which it is legitimate, and to be seen as the most fundamental way of appre-hending the world. Once the success of the scientific worldview within science itself was apparent, philosophers began to interpret the world we experience in its terms. For example, John Locke, the seventeenth-century English empiricist (and himself a scientist as well as a philosopher) argued that we should distinguish between 'primary' and 'secondary' qualities. An entity's primary qualities are those features of the entity which are intrinsic to it. Such qualities as the object's shape and size, or its momentum, for example, are intrinsic to the object, which is to say that they exist whether or not the object is perceived by us. Its secondary qualities, on the other hand, are not intrinsic to the object, but are a product of its relation to us. For example, Locke claimed that an object is not *really* this colour or that. It simply reflects light at varying frequencies, and we perceive this reflected light as colour. If we did not possess the sense organs we do, light would still be reflected by objects at different frequencies, but there would be no call to speak of colour.

Perhaps this seems a little too quick. Why should we think that there is no such thing as colour just because if we did not have eyes we would not see it? After all, we are not tempted to think that physical objects do not exist because if we lacked all senses we could not be aware of their existence. It is not the mere fact that we need specialized sense organs to be aware of colour (or of sound or odour) that makes philosophers like Locke suspicious of the very existence of these qualities. It is instead the fact that we can give a complete explanation of the features of objects which cause us to experience them as coloured without referring to colour at all. We can, that is, reduce colour to the (supposedly) more fundamental vocabulary of science. Think of a planet inhabited by aliens who lack all organs for perceiving light. Imagine that these aliens instead experience their world by sonar, as bats do. These aliens might have a highly developed vocabulary for describing the qualities of the sonar echoes they perceive, akin to our colour vocabulary. They might experience a spectrum of sounds, which they divide up into categories analogous to our colours. Though we can conceive of such a vocabulary, we do not feel tempted to think that these sound colours *really* exist. We have no trouble conceding that what the aliens perceive as qualities are really just vibrations in the air. Similarly, we ought to concede that what we perceive as colours are really just the effect of the surface reflectant properties of physical objects.

We are now well down the road to the objectivist viewpoint. Once one more element is in place, we will have it before us in all its power. It could hardly fail to escape the notice of philosophers that colours, sounds and odours were not the only qualities conspicuous by their absence from the best scientific accounts. Also absent were values, construed widely. We might *experience* the eruption of a volcano as terrifying, but that is simply a fact about our psychological states, not about the volcano. The beauty of a sunset, similarly, is in the eye of the beholder, not in the object perceived. And so on for all values. The world that is real is the world described by science, and it contains nothing corresponding to our values. These values must instead be seen as having their source in us, in our psychological states. They are, essentially, figments of our imagination. We project them upon the world, and then naïvely attribute to them an existence independent of us.

The picture that has emerged is of a universe that consists simply of physical entities obeying causal laws. It is a universe that is indifferent to our plans, our hopes, our desires, simply because at bottom these are no more than hallucinations. Science, in a memorable phrase of Max Weber's, disenchants the world. Its enchantments – the values and meanings that allowed us to take it for a spiritual realm – are shown to be no more than our projected fantasies. The final twist is given to this way of understanding the universe and our place within it when, in the wake of thinkers like Darwin, we begin to suspect that we ourselves are at root to be understood in exactly the same way as the inanimate world. We, too, are merely physical beings; we, too, obey the laws of causality and evolve in response to these laws. Even we, at bottom, are no more meaningful than are the waves and particles of the physicist.

This objectivist view of the universe has proven very powerful and very persuasive. The spectacular success of science, which seems to presuppose something very like this view, certainly accounts for a great deal of its appeal. Its defenders have been able to depict themselves as 'hard-nosed' realists, and accuse their opponents of mere sentimentality. So deeply has the view penetrated our culture that it has begun to take on the unassailability of common sense.

Sartre and objectivism

At first glance it might well seem that Sartre himself ought to be committed to objectivism. After all, the distinction that underlies objectivism, between the objective world as it really is and the merely human world of values, seems to parallel closely the distinction that Sartre insists upon, between being and nothingness, between what he will call the 'in-itself' – the world as it would be without human beings – and the 'for-itself', the being of consciousness. Moreover, as we will see, Sartre, as much as the objectivist, insists that values have their source in our free choice. In some sense, then, he seems committed to the view of values as projected upon an objective world that is fundamentally indifferent to them.

In fact, as we shall see later, Sartre does not avoid the objectivist view entirely. The most important gaps and incoherencies in his thought can be traced to the residual power that view has for him. Yet despite this attraction, Sartre develops a powerful critique of the objectivist view. What problems it poses for him are the result of his not taking to heart the lessons of his own objections to it.

Perhaps Sartre is slow to absorb the full significance of his own best insights because he comes to them relatively late. Though Sartre had attempted to read Heidegger's work on several occasions previously, it was, by his own admission, only at the start of the Second World War that he really began to understand it. And it was Heidegger, above all, who showed Sartre the way beyond the objectivist view.

It was Heidegger's careful description of our 'being-in-the-world' which freed Sartre from the objectivist picture. If we reflect in the proper way on how we experience the world, Heidegger argued, we will see that this experience, and not the scientific picture, is the more fundamental. Imagine yourself engaged in any typically human activity. Heidegger's own famous example is of someone engaged in building something. When I am working with hammer and nails, for example, the hammer does not exist for me *first* as an object in the world, which I only subsequently utilize as an instrument. On the contrary, it exists for me first and foremost as the means whereby I engage in my project. When I am immersed in the ordinary activities of life, Heidegger claims, things are ordinarily revealed to me as *equipment*, as tools. The choice of the hammer as an example is thus no accident; for Heidegger its being is paradigmatic of the way in which the objects that surround me are normally revealed to me. Ordinarily I am barely aware of the hammer *as such*. It exists for me as one element in a broader totality. The hammer is not revealed to me as an independent thing, but as the means whereby I will drive *these* nails into *this* wood for *that* end. The meaning of my act of hammering is for me to find in this future end, for the sake of which I now swing the tool. The hammer takes its place within this totality, and refers me to my end. It is the bookshelf to be built which confers meaning on my use of the tool.

Thus, when I am absorbed in my everyday activity, the objects that surround me do not appear to me as mere *things*. Their being, Heidegger will say, is that of the ready-to-hand. Everything changes, however, when something goes wrong. I strike the nail once more, and the head of the hammer flies off. I am left holding just its handle. I stare down at the piece of metal in my hands. Suddenly it seems to me that it is a mere physical thing, its being akin to those meaningless objects of which the advocate of the scientific view is so fond. Its being is now, Heidegger will say, that of the merely present-at-hand.

One way to make sense of what has happened is to say that while I was caught up in my everyday concerns, I was absorbed in a fantasy of my own making. It seemed to me that I inhabited a world that was meaningful, but only because I failed to see that I myself had created this world and projected meaning on to it. Of course, the universe is indifferent to whether or not my bookshelf exists. From its point of view – imagining for a moment that it could have one – it is all the same whether these pieces of wood are arranged in this manner, or that, or whether they simply rot on the ground. Now, though, I can no longer sustain the illusion. Harsh reality breaks in, and I see the objects for what they really are – mere meaningless things.

This is not how Heidegger interprets what has happened. He asks us to notice, first, the order in which the different kinds of being were revealed to us. My tools existed for me *first* as equipment, as ready-to-hand, and only *subsequently*, when they failed me, did they come to be revealed as present-at-hand. Though this is a long way away from being conclusive evidence, it is, at least, suggestive that the view of things as present-at-hand – that is, as mere meaningless things – is in fact parasitic upon that of them as belonging to a meaningful universe.

Heidegger is here attempting nothing less than a frontal assault on both poles that have dominated philosophy at least since Descartes. He is attempting simultaneously to undermine the view of things as essentially objects, and of human beings as essentially subjects surveying them. These two notions are, as he realizes, correlative; they stand or fall together.[7] Thus far, we have emphasized his attack upon the idea that things exist fundamentally as objects. But the same example can be utilized to show how he attempts to rethink the being of the subject. Traditionally, the subject has been thought of primarily as the subject of *knowledge*. By arguing that philosophy must begin by vanquishing radical doubt, Descartes ensured that philosophy would be centred around epistemology. Moreover, the Cartesian claim that we have indubitable access only to the content of our minds had had the effect of cutting us off from the world and from other people. We are, the Cartesian will say, essentially minds, spiritual substances that only contingently find themselves with physical bodies, and the sole real relationship we can have with the world and with others is the relation of knowing. This tendency to regard ourselves primarily as subjects of knowledge is correlative with the attitude that takes the present-at-hand being of objects as primordial: if objects are most authentically encountered as present-at-hand, then they are fundamentally things to be known, and not equipment with which to come to grips.

Heidegger will decisively undermine the primacy of epistemology. The Cartesian subject was essentially an observing subject, looking out upon a world to which it was foreign. Heidegger's subject, however, is essentially an acting subject. If we try to capture the activity of a carpenter, as she builds a bookshelf, within the Cartesian scheme, we will end up with a caricature of human being-in-the-world. Imagine how the Cartesian must depict the difference between the skilled carpenter and the beginner. Perhaps the beginner will be given a set of instructions, telling her how to hold the hammer, the best place to locate the nails, the order in which the planks ought to be affixed, and so on. She carries out these instructions slowly and clumsily. The skilled carpenter, on the other hand, builds the bookshelf with an ease and fluency altogether lacking in the beginner. The Cartesian will explain the difference by saying that by dint of practice the carpenter has internalized the instructions; she no longer need refer to them because they have become a part of her stock of knowledge.

But this is an implausible picture of the way in which we carry out those activities with which we are most familiar. When we think about just those actions in which we engage most often, we find that it is not the case that we know how to do them in the same way as our imagined apprentice learns how to do carpentry (only better). If that were the case, we should be able to reel off the set of instructions for how to perform these activities. But frequently we cannot do this. Instead, we very often find ourselves at a loss when someone asks us how we perform the tasks at which we are most skilled. If the skilled carpenter is asked how she holds the hammer, she will probably have to pick one up to find out. She will pay attention to what she does, rather than focusing on what she is doing. In other words, she will move from treating the hammer as ready-to-hand, a part of the instrumental complex with which she acts, to present-at-hand. Thus, Heidegger will want to insist, it cannot be the case that relating to objects as present-at-hand, and thus relating to them by knowing them, is primary. Instead, both attitudes are derived from a more fundamental manner of relating to the world. First and foremost, we are actors in the world, and our knowledge of it is derived from this more fundamental activity.

The phenomenologist does not deny that we must know – in some sense – what we are doing in order to be able to do it. The claim is, rather, that the picture of knowledge which Cartesianism has propagated is inappropriate for understanding the kind of knowledge our activity involves. We might usefully compare the claim here to Wittgenstein's remarks on language, in the *Philosophical Investigations*. Speaking a language is a paradigm of the kind of knowledge the phenomenologist has in mind. We speak our first language – and any others we know well – in much the same kind of way as the carpenter hammers. That is, we act without needing to think about how we act; we are concerned with what we want to say, and only peripherally with how we are to say it. We do not refer to the rules of grammar in order to formulate a sentence; we simply speak.

Someone in thrall to the Cartesian picture of knowledge might insist that nevertheless we must know the rules of grammar. If we did not know these rules, then we would make mistakes. Since we do not make mistakes, we must be following the rules. We must have internalized them, to the point where we are no longer conscious of them. We follow them automatically; nevertheless, we still follow them.

Like the phenomenologists, Wittgenstein argues that this is a mistake. Moreover, his account of how the mistake comes about runs closely parallel to theirs. On both accounts, it comes from getting things the wrong way round. On the phenomenological account, the mistake arises when we come to think that the kind of attention we pay to the objects in the world when we step back from our involvement with them and simply regard them as things is primordial. As we have seen, this gives rise to a conception of ourselves as essentially knowing subjects. For Wittgenstein, our mistake with regard to language arises when we take the manner in which we acquire a second language as the model for the way in which we speak our first. Very often, we acquire a second language by learning rules: we are taught how to conjugate verbs, for example, or the way in which the cases modify nouns. Since this is how we acquire a second language, we make the mistake of thinking that we must have acquired our first in a similar way. We are well aware that no one ever actually sat us down when we were babies and taught us the rules of grammar (that kind of explicit teaching comes only much later, after we already are fluent speakers). But we think we must have acquired them nevertheless. Perhaps we gradually came to detect regularities in the sentences we heard, and we abstracted the grammatical rules from these regularities.

Wittgenstein and the phenomenologists reject this picture. It is profoundly misleading, in so far as it gives rise to the temptation to think that when we speak a language fluently we are following its rules, just as a beginner does (only much more quickly). It leads us, that is, to take language for one more present-at-hand entity, which must be analysed and dissected in order to be understood. Taking language apart is a perfectly legitimate activity, an activity that might allow us to acquire knowledge that is not to be had in any other way. The scientific viewpoint is valid and useful, its successes in allowing us to predict and control the world are great. But it is a great mistake to think that the way of knowing upon which it relies is or ought to be the sole way of knowing. It is, in fact, derivative, from a more primordial manner of being in the world. We are first actors who are engaged in the world, before we are knowers who contemplate it.

A human world

Thus the phenomenologist, at least the phenomenologist of the post-Heideggerian variety, is committed to two fundamental, closely related theses, which concern the manner in which we exist in the world:

1. We are fundamentally engaged with the world; we act in it before we contemplate it.
2. The entities in the world are revealed to us primarily as equipment, in an extended sense. They have a place in our projects before they are mere extended matter.

The great prestige of the scientific viewpoint has obscured the truth of these theses from us; we misunderstand our own being in the world and take ourselves for disinterested spectators, because we believe that our engagements are at bottom no more than subjective projections. In fact, this is to get things exactly backwards. Objectivity is not the fundamental manner in which being is revealed to us; instead, it is a derived manner of being, which we reveal when we step back from our involvement in the world and its instrumental complexes.

What are the consequences of this phenomenological stance towards the world and ourselves? Most fundamentally, it implies that we live in a world that is *meaningful*. Meanings – values, the traces of human projects – are not imposed upon objects; instead, objects are revealed to us through their meanings. The world is not divided up into discrete entities, independent of our choice. Things do not naturally begin *here* and end *there*. Why, for example, do we assume that a tree is a fundamental unit, an entity complete unto itself? Why should the fundamental unit not be the leaf, on the one hand, or the forest, on the other? The phenomenological answer will be that it is our manner of being in the world, our projects and plans, which articulates the world in this manner rather than that. The tree appears to me as a source of wood, for example; it takes a definite shape in my world. It stands out as an individuated object, against the forest that becomes background for it. In the same manner, Sartre notes, the crag is revealed to the climber as a separate object only in and through the project of climbing it: 'the rock is carved out on the ground of the world by the effect of the initial choice of my freedom' (BN, p. 488). In general, things are only revealed to me as being what they are, possessing the qualities they do, in terms of my projects.

But if it is the case that the world is articulated into discrete objects in terms of our projects and practical concerns, why is there so much agreement upon what objects there are? There are two reasons for this widespread agreement. First, if it is indeed true that the world is divided up into objects in terms of human projects, then we ought to expect a great deal of agreement. For, as Sartre himself insisted, though there is no shared human nature, 'there is nevertheless a human universality of *condition*' (EH, p. 362). We share a biology, which imposes certain tasks upon all of us. We must all solve the problems of how to find shelter and how to feed ourselves; we must all learn to make sense of the facts of birth and death. Given this fact, and given the fact that our projects only *reveal* the world and are powerless to *create* it, we ought to expect a great deal of cross-cultural similarity.

The second reason for this widespread agreement as to what are the basic components of the universe has to do with the fact that none of us is ever confronted with the task of articulating our surroundings from scratch. Instead, we are all born into ongoing cultural entities, which divide up existence for us. We are, Sartre says, born into a world that is already inhabited by meaning-conferring creatures. Thus, 'I find myself engaged in an *already meaningful* world which reflects to me meanings which I have not put into it' (BN, p. 510). These are meanings that objects have independently of me, and which I have no choice but simply to accept, the meanings of a particular society: 'I am thrown into a worker's world, a French world ... which offers me its meanings without my having done anything to disclose them' (BN, p. 514).

Let us revert to our earlier example in order to see how cultures might individuate the world. As we saw, the rock reveals itself as a separate entity, a rock 'to-be-climbed', in terms of someone's project of climbing it. We now see that we can go further than this. Our explanation of how it is that the world comes to be articulated in one way, and not another, does not have to come to an abrupt end as soon as we note that its divisions are the result of a project; we can attempt to explain the project itself. Mountain climbing is the kind of activity that arises only in certain kinds of societies. It might be explained by the fact that the society in question values risk-taking behaviour, for instance. Or it might be explained by some mystical or religious significance being conferred on high places: we can well imagine that standing on the peak of some mountain is held to give one privileged access to heavenly spirits. If you are born into a society in which either of these is the case, then it is far more likely that high peaks will stand out for you. If, on the other hand, you are born into a rather more prosaic society, in which activities are held to be valuable only in so far as they contribute to material well-being, and risk taking is seen as a selfish extravagance, then it is far more likely that the distant mountains will be nothing more than the background against which one lives and objects appear.

A proponent of the objectivist view need not deny any of this. She might well agree that different societies confer different significances upon the objects of the world. For some, mountains are highly significant objects, for others mere background. Some are interested in the natural world, and identify thousands of plants and insects, others have only broad categories into which to divide them. But, the objectivist might insist, this very fact demonstrates the profound importance of the objectivist position. The meaning conferred upon the entities of the world might vary according to our purposes and our culture; so much she might accept. But the basic structure of that world itself is not subject to variation. Since the meaning conferred upon it varies, we are justified in ignoring this level. It is, as the objectivist has always insisted, merely subjective. We ought to shift our focus away from these ephemeral meanings, and concentrate instead on the unchanging substratum that bears them. It is this substratum, the level of brute matter, which is the support of all these meanings, and it is this which alone deserves to be called truly real. For it is this level alone which would continue to exist in the absence of all human purposes and projects.

Sartre does not deny that this is so; that is, he does not deny that there must be a substratum of matter which bears the human meanings with which he is concerned. The rock is revealed to me as an entity to be climbed, but it is beyond my power to vary its steepness; 'what my freedom can not determine is whether the rock "to be scaled" will or will not lend itself to scaling. This is part of the brute being of the rock' (BN, p. 488). What he does deny, however, is that we can claim sensibly to be concerned with the stuff of the universe as it is, independently of our purposes and projects. Things are always necessarily known from a perspective; the world is necessarily revealed to me from where I am. For me, the glass is to the left of the decanter and behind it, whereas for you it is on the right and in front. We cannot do as the objectivist would have us, and be concerned only with where it is in-itself, without reference to me or to you, because it is only anywhere *at all* in relation to us:

> It is not even conceivable that a consciousness could survey the world in such a way that the glass could be *simultaneously* given to it at the right and at the left of the decanter, in front of it and behind it ... because this fusion of right and left, of before and behind, would result in the total disappearance of 'thises' at the heart of a primitive indistinction. (BN, p. 306)

If it somehow came about that the things of the world were to appear to us without distinction of here and there, near and far, and so on, we would no longer be able to distinguish anything from anything else. We could not speak of tree and forest, of foreground and background, because everything would be swept up into a vast confusion. We would perceive everything simultaneously, but, since we would be unable to distinguish anything, this would be equivalent to perceiving nothing at all. Thus perception is necessarily situated; we perceive the world as divided up in this way or that, or we fail to perceive it at all.

It follows from this, Sartre claims, that the objectivist project, of grasping the world as it really is without reference to the meanings that our purposes confer upon it, is incoherent:

> The point of view of pure knowledge is contradictory; there is only the point of view of engaged knowledge. This amounts to saying that knowledge and action are only two abstract aspects of an original concrete relation. (BN, p. 308)

It is simply false to think that we inhabit the world that science reveals, the world of brute matter, alien and indifferent, upon which we subsequently project meanings. Instead, we inhabit an inherently meaningful world, a world of significance.

We can drive home the point using a piece of terminology that Sartre borrows from Kurt Lewin to describe the geography of our world. Our world is 'hodological'; its space is mapped in terms of human needs and interests. '[H]uman-reality is that by which something we can call place comes to things' (BN, p. 490). That is, the world is not *first* a meaningless space of exteriority, upon which a human significance comes to be imposed. It is, from the moment that we exist, a space of meaning and we map it accordingly. Once again, the objectivist who would assert the precedence of their perspective has got things the wrong way round: the objectivist perspective is a stance that we can take up only because we are able (temporarily) to step back from our involvement in the world and imagine what it might have been like if we had never existed.

This geographical – in an extended sense of the word – example is a particularly clear case of the primacy of a significant world over a purely objective one, in that it concerns so many of the concepts central to the manner in which we locate ourselves in space. Sartre's point here might be understood as the claim that such geographical terms ought to be understood on the model of indexical expressions; that is, words that alter their meaning according to the context in which they are used. In the geographical case, we often have recourse to such indexicals as 'here' and 'there'. Obviously, these terms have a reference that is relative to the context in which they are used. Something which is 'here' for me may well be 'there' for you. Similarly, words like 'close' and 'distant' get their reference from context.

No one would deny that 'near' and 'distant' are indexicals, in the sense that their reference alters according to where I am. If I am in Paris then the Eiffel Tower is near, but it does not remain near when I am in Rome. Sartre's distinctive claim is not that these terms are to be understood in relation to their context of use, but that they vary *phenomenologically*, in the sense of 'phenomenology' that we have been using. That is, what gives content to these indexicals is not any objective measure ('The Eiffel Tower is near to me, since it is five hundred metres from me', or something similar); instead, it is the context of lived experience which does the work. From this point of view, to say something is 'near' to me is not to say that it is less than a certain number of metres away from where I am. Instead, it is to say that I could reach it easily, or quickly, or perhaps that it is familiar to me (it exists as a well-defined region on my hodological map). Thus, to use one of Sartre's own examples, a city that is located twenty miles away from the village in which I live but which is connected to it by public transport, is much nearer to me, phenomenologically, than is the inaccessible mountain peak that looms eight hundred metres above my head. The *objective* relative closeness of the latter does not alter the fact that it is hodologically very far from me. The peak is off my hodological map, and so it exists at a great distance for me.

Distance, and place in general, is thus *primordially* measured in terms of lived experience, and not in terms of objective units. This is something we all implicitly acknowledge when we measure distance in *time*. If I ask you how far it is to the post office, you might legiti-mately respond by mentioning units not of distance but of time: 'About ten minutes.' Moreover, your response might well be rather more useful to me than would be one couched in purely objective terms. 'Ten minutes' walk' will mean more to me than would 'one and a half kilometres'.

Notice that to say that distances are meaningful hodologically, in terms of their place in my life with its plans and projects, is to imply that distance can vary as the kinds of activities and options available to me change. Two hundred years ago, Australia was eight months' sailing from Great Britain. Today it is less than twenty-four hours' flying away. The distance, as measured in objective units, has not changed, but in hodological terms the two countries have drawn much closer.

The objectivist will insist that this is all so much romantic nonsense; that it mistakes the overlay of meaning that we project on to the world for what is really there. The distance between London and Sydney is as great as it ever was; all that has changed is our means of traversing it. Sartre is not denying the fact that, as measured in kilometres, the distance has remained the same. What he is insisting on is that these objective units have their origin in the very plans and projects, the meaningful world, that they are subsequently used to denigrate. Objective units of measure and the maps and navigational instruments that utilize them are *useful*, Sartre agrees. But it is this very usefulness which accounts both for their origin and for the significance they have for us. Because I live in a world that I comprehend hodologically, a map that shows the distance between two towns I have never visited is meaningful to me; I understand it by comparing it with distances I *have* traversed. We make and understand maps because we live in a world that is understood hodologically; the lived experience precedes and provides access to the objective, and not the other way round.

Thus my understanding of objective distance presupposes my lived experience of distance, and is therefore parasitic on the latter. It might seem, however, that this claim is open to a counter-example. Not all maps show distances I could experience, even in principle. We construct maps, and otherwise measure distances, not only between features on the surface of the world, but also between astronomical entities: stars, galaxies, black holes, and so on. I certainly cannot understand the distance, measured in light years, between two stars in terms of my experience of having traversed such spans. Much the same kind of thing might be said about the very small distances between microscopic entities. Here too my experience of traversing distances provides me with no guide to the measurements being made. Yet we understand such measurements, do we not?

I think it is plausible to claim that most of us do not truly understand the distances involved in these cases. Do you really comprehend what it means to say that two stars are separated by ninety light years? I suspect that all it means to you (as to me) is that they are a long way apart. This is not, however, to say that an astronomer cannot understand the claim. He will, in fact, understand it hodologically. Just as I understand the distances involved when someone says that two towns are twelve kilometres apart, because I have often driven comparable distances, so he understands astronomical distances because he works with them constantly. He understands them, therefore, not in terms of the time it would take him to travel the distance, but in terms of their place in his experience of astronomy. Space for him is mapped hodologically, and the objective mapping is comprehensible for him only because it is so mapped.

Let me conclude this sketch of the manner in which the world we experience is a meaningful one by recounting a story that Sartre tells in *Being and Nothingness*:

> The story is told of an emigrant who was going to leave France for Argentina after the failure of his political party: When someone remarked to him that Argentina was 'very far away,' he asked, 'Far from what?' (BN, p. 494)

This story neatly encapsulates the point Sartre has been elaborating, that distances are meaningful only in relation to our projects. For someone who centres their life around France, Argentina is 'very far away'. For this person, France constitutes the centre of their hodological map, and it will be in relation to that centre that other places are understood. Another country will be comprehended, first and foremost, as more or less distant from France (where 'distant' is understood phenomenologically, that is, not only in terms of kilometres, but also in terms of culture and language). For an internationalist, on the other hand, the world will have no centre; Argentina will not be 'far away', because there is nowhere from which it can be distant. The protagonist of Sartre's story, however, is not an internationalist, and for him distance is understood in yet a third manner. France had been the centre of this man's plans. Now, however, they have failed, and France can no longer function as his focus. But no new project has yet arisen to take its place. Perhaps he will succeed in refocusing his life around Argentina; for the moment, however, it is neither near nor far, for the reference points in terms of which he measured proximity have collapsed.

Quality as the revelation of being

I have concentrated, thus far, on our understanding of the physical space of our world, in order to clarify the way in which we live in a world that is meaningful, and the manner in which the objective standpoint can arise and be comprehensible only on the basis of this lived experience. I will now situate this point within a broader Sartrean theme: opposition to analysis.

In the manner in which Sartre uses the term, 'analysis' refers to the attempt to understand things by breaking them down into their component parts. It is precisely in this project that the objectivist is engaged. Thus, she argues that we have not understood a phenomenon until we have seen how it is constructed out of more basic elements. We understand a cloud when we know that it is composed of water droplets; we understand water, in turn, when we realize that it is composed of hydrogen and oxygen, and so on.

There is no denying the power of the analytical approach to understanding nature. Understanding the chemical or the physical composition of the entities that make up the world represents a considerable advance in human knowledge; moreover, an advance with immensely important implications for our ability to predict and control the world. As with all such objectivist innovations, Sartre does not deny the value of such knowledge, in its proper place. Instead, what he objects to is the illegitimate extension of this manner of understanding things beyond the realm in which it has proved valuable, to the world as it is lived and experienced.

Thus, taken in by the power and prestige of the analytical methods of the natural sciences, we might attempt to analyse our everyday behaviour in the same kind of way: by breaking it down to the simple components out of which it is allegedly built. The British empiricist philosophers, such as John Locke, attempted something of this sort, and it remains the dominant way of understanding human behaviour in psychology. Roughly, the path taken by this version of the objectivist approach is to understand complex 'ideas'

– where this word is taken as encompassing both the products of imagination and the data of perception – as built up out of simple ideas. For Locke, these were ultimately derived from perception, but nothing turns on this point so far as the analytical approach is concerned: complex ideas might equally be built out of simple ideas that are innate, or out of a combination of innate and empirically derived ideas. For our purposes, the important point is that complex ideas – which is to say, almost all of them – are held to be fully understood only if they are broken down into component parts.

Thus, for example, if I am fully to comprehend my perception of the most ordinary object, I must see how it is built up out of simpler perceptions (and perhaps other, more abstract ideas as well). Thus, when I look down at my shirt, I see a blue fabric. This composite perception is built out of a number of simple ideas which are the deliverances of my senses. It is composed out of the perception of the blueness of the fabric, plus its texture, for example. The concrete perception is the product of the addition of these elements.

Sartre denies that this objectivist depiction of perception will ever allow us to grasp our own experience. He denies, that is, that we reconstitute the concrete perception out of its component parts. The reason we cannot do so is that, once again, the objectivist has things wrong way round. She thinks to reach the concrete by following the route that, she holds, the brain itself must have taken. What she fails to see is that the components out of which the perception is supposedly built do not exist before the perception. In fact, they become accessible to us only *through* the perception. We do not see blueness, plus a certain texture: instead, we see *this* fabric, and subsequently we can, if we like, break down our perception of this fabric into different elements. The fact that we can so analyse the perception into different components does not imply that the perception itself was built up out of these components, any more than the fact that we can separate the yolk from the white of an egg shows that eggs are constructed by adding yolk to white.

Perception is not built up out of simpler elements. The truth is the other way round: these simpler elements can be abstracted from perception, but the procedure cannot be reversed. That is, though we can break down my perception into an idea of blueness and another of a certain texture, we cannot go in the other direction, building the perception out of these elements. The idea of this blueness plus the idea of this texture do not equal this concrete perception. This is so, Sartre argues, because the truth is that I do not perceive generic blueness when I see the shirt. Instead, I see *this* blueness only as it exists *here*, on *this* shirt. The texture of the fabric helps constitute the colour I see, just as the colour helps shape my experience of the texture. I do not see blue; I see *textured fabric blue*; the two qualities are not distinct, but interpenetrate each other. The perception I have is of an organized totality, not of two separate elements that are then combined.

Sartre makes this point with regard not to the perception of fabric, but to the manner in which foods are experienced. In this example, the colour and the flavour of the food are inseparable:

> If I eat a pink cake, the taste of it is pink; the light sugary perfume, the oiliness of the butter cream *are* the pink. Thus I eat the pink as I see the sugary [*sic*]. (BN, p. 615)

My experience of the cake is not built up out of its taste, plus its colour, plus its texture. Instead, it is exactly the other way round: these elements are accessible to me only by a process of abstraction from the concrete totality as it is given to me. Just as, in the case of my experience of the physical world, the lived meaning precedes the objectively measurable facts, so here the perception of the totality precedes the component parts. In both cases, we are tempted to think that the lived experience is somehow built on the basis of the objective, whereas in fact it is the latter which is derived from the former. We live in a thoroughly meaningful world; a world that is made up of concrete totalities, all of which have significance for our projects and plans. The objective world of science is not the foundation of this world; it is instead itself derived from it.

FURTHER READING

There are several good introductory books on phenomenology. I have found Michael Hammond, Jane Howarth and Russell Keat, *Understanding Phenomenology* (Oxford: Blackwell, 1991) particularly useful. Dermot Moran's *Introduction to Phenomenology* (New York: Routledge, 2000) is rather more advanced.

The fact/value distinction, and the idea that values can always be reduced to facts, has its origin with the British empiricists. Its best-known statement is probably in David Hume's *A Treatise of Human Nature* (Oxford: Clarendon Press, 1967; originally published in 1739). For further reading on this topic, and on the distinction between primary and secondary qualities, see J.L. Mackie's *Problems from Locke* (Oxford: Clarendon Press, 1976).

Heidegger's arguments for the priority of the lived world over the objective are elaborated in *Being and Time*, trans. John Macquarrie and Edward Robinson (Oxford: Basil Blackwell, 1962). *Being and Time* is, however, a dense and difficult work. Perhaps the best guide to the sections that concern us is Hubert L. Dreyfus's *Being-in-the-World* (Cambridge, MA: MIT Press, 1992). Dreyfus has continued the phenomenological attack on the objective point of view in his *What Computers Still Can't Do*, where the target is artificial intelligence. David Cooper's *Existentialism: A Reconstruction*, 2nd edn (Oxford, Blackwell, 1999) is clear and illuminating on the critique of objectivism.

Wittgenstein's attack on the notion that expertise in speaking a language consists in mastery of a set of rules runs throughout his *Philosophical Investigations*, trans. G.E.M. Anscombe (Oxford: Basil Blackwell, 1958). For an exposition of Wittgenstein's argument by someone sympathetic to phenomenology, see Charles Taylor's 'To Follow a Rule', in *Philosophical Arguments* (Cambridge, MA: Havard University Press, 1995).

Chapter Two

In-itself, for-itself and for-others: Sartre's ontology

We now know what Sartre means when he claims that his ontology will be phenomenological. It is now time to begin sketching that ontology itself. What, according to Sartre, is the fundamental nature of reality?

The in-itself and the for-itself

Sartre argues that the universe is made up of two fundamentally different kinds of things. The 'in-itself' corresponds roughly to Descartes' extended substance: it refers to all the material entities in the universe. For Sartre, whatever is in-itself simply *is*. It is a plenitude of being: 'It is what it is … it can encompass no negation. It is full positivity' (BN, p. xlii). To say that the in-itself simply is what it is, without possibility of negation, is to say that there is a fundamental sense in which it can never be modified: what is in-itself can never be created or destroyed, damaged or improved. What can Sartre mean by making this claim? Surely it is simply obvious that material entities can undergo change? He cannot mean to deny that if I drop a glass, it will most likely shatter?

Sartre is not denying that this kind of change comes about. He holds, however, that the shattering of the glass is a change *for me* – for the observer – and not for the glass considered simply as in-itself. To make this clear, think of some enormous upheaval rending the surface of an uninhabited planet – perhaps one of those storms that perpetually rage on the surface of Jupiter. Strictly speaking, Sartre would suggest, there is no destruction here. All that there really is, from the point of view of the in-itself, is the rearrangement of the constituent particles of the surface of the planet. For there to be destruction, there would need to be an observer, something that was not in-itself, but was instead for-itself. Something that is for-itself is defined by the fact that it exists in relation to itself; that is, riven by an inner duality. Such a being is capable – for reasons we shall explore shortly – of assuming a particular perspective on the world of the in-itself, of *valuing* it. Since the for-itself can value the in-itself, the for-itself has an interest in what happens to the in-itself. From the perspective of such a being, there can be destruction or, for that matter, improvement: a storm can bring ruin or the rain can replenish the parched earth. It is only for a for-itself that the in-itself can be negated.

A for-itself, as by now is obvious, is the kind of being that we all are. Thus it corresponds roughly to Descartes' thinking substance. Hence Sartre's claim is equivalent to saying that destruction, and not only the destruction for which we are causally responsible like that which results from war, but even the destruction that results from natural phenomena like tornadoes and fires, comes to the world from us, from human beings. Since it is we, and we alone, who value our cities and our farms, or for that matter even the natural beauties of forests and wild places, it only *for us* that these things are destroyed. From the perspective of the in-itself, nothing is ever destroyed; it is simply rearranged:

> In a sense, certainly, man is the only being by whom a destruction can be accomplished. A geological plication, a storm, do not destroy – or at least they do not destroy *directly*; they merely modify the distribution of masses of beings. There is no *less* after the storm than before. There is *something else* … Thus it is man who renders cities destructible, precisely because he posits them as fragile and precious … *it is man* who destroys his cities through the agency of earthquakes or directly. (BN, pp. 8–9)

We see, therefore, that it is because the for-itself *values* the world that it can be destroyed or degraded. The for-itself, Sartre will say, is the origin of negation.

We can now begin to make initial sense of the title of Sartre's book. The in-itself corresponds to the first word of the title, 'Being' ('Being is. Being is in-itself. Being is what it is' [p. xlii]), whereas the for-itself corresponds to the second word. The for-itself is the origin of all the nothingness that is in the universe, since it is only for it that there can be destruction.

We have seen that it is because the for-itself can value being that, for it, being can be destroyed. This might suggest that the valuing is primary and the negation is secondary. In fact, it is the other way round: the for-itself is able to value things only because it is the origin of all negation. What accounts for this extraordinary ability of the for-itself, to produce nothingness? Sartre suggests we take that question – in fact, *any* question – as the 'guiding thread' (p. 4) in our inquiry. We can interrogate the question itself, and see what it presupposes.

To be able to question something, Sartre claims, we need to be able to reflect upon it. But we can reflect upon something only if we are at a distance from it, just as a mirror can reflect an object only if that object is distinct from it. Thus the ability to question something presupposes that we can take a certain distance from what we question. We must be distinguishable from that which we question in order that we can question it. This is the case even if what we are questioning is ourselves. Think, for example, of someone trying to decide what he should do with his life. This person might well take towards himself exactly the same kind of attitude as someone else might take towards him. That is, he might examine his interests, his behaviour and his abilities in order to see what kind of life he is suited for and might enjoy. He might utilize exactly the same sorts of information that could be available to anyone else. In order to be able to question himself, he must step back from himself, treat himself as an object.

Our ability to question ourselves is a defining characteristic of the for-itself. The for-itself is, precisely, *for*-itself; that is, it exists at a distance from itself. It is internally fissured, in such a manner that it is capable of adopting an attitude to itself, of treating itself as an object. Or in other words, the for-itself is a being that is separated from itself. But what separates the for-itself from itself?

Whatever intervenes between the for-itself and itself cannot, Sartre says, be anything in-itself. The for-itself is of a radically different kind of being to the in-itself, and the in-itself cannot inhabit it. As we shall see, nothing can inhabit consciousness. What separates the for-itself from itself, then? The answer is, precisely, nothing. That is, the for-itself is separated from itself by a negation; the negation that it secretes, and which allows it to take a distance from itself, to question itself.

The for-itself is capable of questioning itself because it is separated from itself by a nothingness. In exactly the same manner, the for-itself is able to ask questions of the world because it is separated from the in-itself by nothingness. Anything that is in-itself exists in a series of causal relations with the rest of the in-itself. In order to be able to turn back on the in-itself, it is necessary to be able to extract oneself from that causal series. This the for-itself can do, because a nothingness separates it from all causes; the ability to question is itself evidence of this separation:

> every question supposes that we realize a nihilating withdrawal in relation to the given … It is essential therefore that the questioner have the permanent possibility of dissociating himself from the causal series which constitutes being and which can produce only being. (BN, p. 23)

The for-itself is separated from itself by a nothingness, and this nothingness which, in a sense, it is enables it to withdraw from the world of the in-itself and question it. Nothingness comes to the world from the for-itself, because the for-itself is its own nothingness. '*The being by which Nothingness comes to the world must be its own Nothingness*' (p. 23).

Nothingness and the question have an even more intimate relation than we have yet suggested. Not only does the nothingness that the for-itself secrete enable it to question the world and itself, this nothingness itself must be perpetually *in question*. If it were not itself in question, then it would have the same kind of stability as the in-itself. It would itself *be*, and to be is to be in-itself. Because Sartre identifies the for-itself with this nothingness which lies at its heart, for him the for-itself is the being whose being is perpetually in question.

These two categories, the for-itself and the in-itself, are the most fundamental in Sartre's ontology. Before we turn to the third, it is therefore worth pausing a moment to consider the extent to which the basis of this ontology is really phenomenological. As you will recall, Sartre is insistent that the world in which we live is a world of significance; one in which meaning is simply and irreducibly *there*. We encounter meaning, we do not impose it. The view that meaning is projected upon inert and indifferent matter gets things backwards. In fact, though we can indeed regard matter as lifeless and meaningless, this view is a perspective that we might take up for a certain purpose. It is not, as the objectivist believes, the fundamental truth about reality; it is derived from and made possible by our more basic experience of a thoroughly meaningful world.

But now Sartre has sketched an ontology that seems to make just the objectivist mistake. It depicts matter – the in-itself – as fundamentally meaningless, and instead holds that meaning only comes to the world with the advent of the for-itself. On this view, meanings end up looking very much like the projections of the objectivist. Has Sartre forgotten his own lessons?

I think we must be careful before we condemn Sartre's ontology on phenomenological grounds. The objectivist mistake does not lie merely in thinking that matter without human beings (or some other conscious beings) is meaningless. That is surely a plausible view. Nothing could matter if there was no one for whom it could matter. No, the objectivist mistake is to think that the world as it *is*, populated by conscious beings, is nevertheless a meaningless world. The objectivist regards the meanings she finds as fundamentally subjective and therefore as 'not really there'. She thinks that to the extent we persist in finding the world a place of significance, we are deceiving ourselves, or are caught in a web of fantasy of our own weaving. Thus the objectivist believes that a true and a complete description of our world will not mention any 'merely human' significances.

This, it ought to be apparent, is not Sartre's position. Instead, he believes that the world we experience is, irreducibly, meaningful. These meanings may have their origin in us, but that is not to say that they are mere projections, which we could strip away, even in imagination. Nor is it to say that because they come from us, they are not real. We are tempted to think that anything that is added to reality by our presence must be, for that very reason, less real than the brute matter that would persist in being even if we had never existed. But this belief is a mere objectivist prejudice. The recognition that values and meanings come to the universe through us should not tempt us into thinking that they are not really real.

Perhaps this will all be somewhat clearer if we compare the significances we encounter in the world to perspectives. We always and necessarily see whatever we examine from some perspective or other. It is certainly true, however, that perspective only comes to the world with us. The notion of a perspective upon the world entails that there is some conscious being whose perspective it is (at least potentially). Noticing this fact, we might be tempted to think that a true description of the world is one that would describe it as it would be seen from no perspective at all. After all, seeing things from a perspective can be distorting, as we all know.

But the fact is there is no such thing as a description of something from no perspective whatsoever. Perceiving something requires taking a perspective. We can grasp this just by examining completely ordinary perceptions. I always see the objects that surround me from one perspective or another. For example, when I look at my desk its undersurface is obscured, as are its legs. I could, of course, change my angle of vision, and look at it from below. Then I would indeed see its undersurface and its legs, but now the desktop would be hidden from me. There is no perspective from which I can see every surface of the entire desk simultaneously. But now imagine what it would be like if it were possible to take up a position from which I could see every part of my desk at once, all equally well. How would I know what it is that I am looking at? How would I know its shape? All I would perceive, if perception like this were possible, would be a wild confusion of angles and colours. I would not be able to make my way about in a world I perceived from no perspective at all.

Just as, though it is true that perspective comes to the world from us, we cannot hope to perceive, or even coherently imagine perceiving, the world as seen from no perspective at all, so it is true that though significance comes to the world through us, we cannot imagine a world without significance. Thus, though Sartre can agree with the objectivist about the origin of our values, nevertheless he can continue to maintain that the objectivist project of describing the world without 'merely human' significances is a fantasy.

Nevertheless, I suspect that Sartre's insistence on the analytical distinction between the in-itself and the meaningful world in which we find ourselves is evidence that he hadn't shaken himself entirely free of the objectivist picture. We must remember that this picture has a strong grip on our imaginations; it is deeply entrenched in Western culture and has been for three hundred years. Though Sartre was intellectually convinced of the validity of the phenomenological case, as yet he had not grasped its full implications. He remained tempted by the picture of a meaningless world, upon which meanings are projected and from which they can in turn be stripped away.

In *Nausea*, Sartre's famous first novel, and a work widely regarded as encapsulating the philosophy of *Being and Nothingness* in a fictionalized form, Sartre's continuing commitment to this objectivist picture is clear. The 'nausea' of the title seems in fact to be nothing more than the experience of the in-itself. This is brought out in the famous passage in which the protagonist, Roquentin, suddenly finds himself confronted by the sheer fact of existence, in the form of a chestnut tree in a park:

> all of a sudden, there it was, as clear as day: existence had suddenly unveiled itself. It had lost its harmless appearance as an abstract category: it was the very stuff of things, that root was steeped in existence. Or rather the root, the park gates, the bench, the sparse grass on the lawn, all that had vanished; the diversity of things, their individuality, was only an appearance, a veneer. This veneer had melted, leaving soft monstrous masses, in disorder – naked, with a frightening, obscene nakedness.[8]

In this almost mystical experience, the significances of the everyday suddenly fall away for Roquentin, and pure in-itself is revealed. All the categories, relations, meanings upon which Sartre the phenomenologist insists, everything that makes our world a thoroughly humanized place, are stripped away:

> It was in vain that I tried to *count* the chestnut trees, to *situate* them in relation to the Velleda, to compare their height with the height of the plane trees: each of them escaped from the relationship in which I tried to enclose it, isolated itself, overflowed. I was aware of the arbitrary nature of these relationships, which I insisted on maintaining in order to delay the collapse of the human world of measures, of quantities, of bearings; they no longer had any grip on things.[9]

The 'absurdity' of all these imposed significances is revealed: pure contingency is uncovered.

I do not wish to claim that the experience that Roquentin undergoes in the municipal park in Bouville is literally impossible. In fact, such experiences may indeed occur. But if Sartre the phenomenologist – as opposed to Sartre the novelist – is right that we live in an irreducibly meaningful world, then the experience cannot have the significance that he seems to attribute to it. Roquentin, and implicitly Sartre himself, seems to take the experience as revealing our true position in the universe. He seems to think that it shows that our social world, with its values and significances, is really a thin veneer, projected on to the indifferent surface of a universe to which it is fundamentally alien. It is not the world of values and meanings which is the true world; it is this cold and meaningless in-itself which is the truth of reality. To the extent we find ourselves at home in the world, we deceive ourselves. But, as we have seen, this is nothing but the objectivist fantasy. In this and similar passages of *Nausea*, Sartre has forgotten (or perhaps not yet learned) the fundamental lesson of existential phenomenology. The cold and indifferent world of the objectivist is not our real world; it is merely a derived perspective we can take on it. And the experience Roquentin undergoes, in which the world appears to him as meaningless, is not the revelation of its true being; it is, instead, the symptom of a pathology. It reflects his alienation from the world, not our real place within it.

Being-for-others

Though Sartre's division of the world into in-itself and for-itself is intended to be exhaustive, there is a third ontological, or perhaps quasi-ontological, category which he introduces in *Being and Nothingness*. Human beings, Sartre has shown, are the kinds of being who exist for-themselves. Yet being-for-itself is a fundamentally reflexive category: only the entity whose being it is can witness it. It appears only to the self whose being it is. Thus other people cannot directly bear witness to my being-for-myself. Yet, as we all well know, this does not imply that they can regard me as simply a thing, a mere in-itself. It is normally impossible to take towards a living human being the kind of attitudes we take toward inanimate objects. Thus, when another person looks at me, a third kind of being arises in the world. This third kind of being Sartre calls 'being-for-others'.

We can witness the birth of this category of being, and grasp the profound implications it will have for our lives, by following Sartre's phenomenological description of the manner in which someone might come to experience *shame*. Sartre begins by asking us to imagine him staring through a keyhole, attempting to spy on the person on the other side of the door. At this point, he is alone, and his attention is fixed upon what he is looking at. Given the facts of the intentionality of consciousness, nothing inhabits his consciousness other than what he is looking at. In particular,

> there is no self to inhabit my consciousness, nothing therefore to which I can refer my acts in order to qualify them. They are in no way *known*; I *am my acts* and hence they carry in themselves their whole justification. I am a pure consciousness *of* things. (BN, p. 259)

All of a sudden, however, he hears footsteps down the hall, and feels the gaze of another person on his back. All of a sudden, everything changes. From being an acting freedom, he suddenly becomes an object within the world – within *someone else's world*. Suddenly he is imbued with qualities, with a character. He is now a *kind* of person; a voyeur, perhaps. From being pure consciousness, he now becomes a self.

Thus, Sartre claims, we each become a self, we acquire our personal identity, by means of the gaze of another. So long as we are alone, we do not possess a stable kernel to which our acts can be referred; as soon as we are looked at, we each become a person among others. We have acquired a new dimension of being.

When I am seen by another, my body, my acts, my quirks and foibles all acquire an *outside*. No longer is my body merely the most intimate of tools, always ready-to-hand. Now it is also an object in the external world. Worse, I myself am now such an object. Whereas before I was a pure freedom, a transcendence of any situation, now I am a 'transcendence transcended', a transcendence become an object for another transcendence. My freedom is now an object for someone else.

Thus I now exist as an object for the gaze of another. I have an outside, a body, a personality, all of which is more accessible to others than it is to myself. It is only by means of these others that I will learn what I am – one cannot be ugly or beautiful, intelligent, mean, and so on, except for-others. Worst of all, I cannot but admit that this being-for-others, this dimension of my being to which I always have imperfect and mediated access, is nevertheless *me*. I *am* my being-for-others. My very experience of shame bears witness to this fact. I can only be ashamed of what is intimately mine, of what I am responsible for:

> Shame is by nature *recognition*. I recognise that I *am* as the Other sees me … Thus the Other has not only revealed to me what I was; he has established me in a new type of being. (BN, p. 222)

Thus I acquire an irreducible and undeniable mode of being by way of the gaze of another. I, who was pure freedom, pure subjectivity, acquire an objectivity in the world. I come to have a *nature* for that other, in so far as they can begin to observe my behaviour, sketch my character and, on that basis, predict my future actions. Thus:

> If there is an Other … I have an outside, I have a *nature*. My original fall is the existence of the Other. (BN, p. 263)

Of course, I do not *really* possess a nature. The gaze of another is not able really to modify my being. Nevertheless, to the extent that I am an object within someone else's world, I appear as a relatively stable and predictable being. My possibilities become calculable *probabilities*, my actions relatively predictable and manipulable. To become an object for others is to become degraded; I, who was pure freedom, have become a mere thing.

If I can undergo these modifications in my being, however, then so can any for-itself. Thus I can always hope to reverse the gaze, to look back at the person who looks at me. If I am successful, I can transcend their transcendence in turn. My subjectivity can burst forth once more, and it will be my erstwhile objectifier who will become the object. For the Sartre of *Being and Nothingness*, all human relations can be resolved into this sinister dialectic of looking-at and being looked-at, of objectifying and being objectified in turn. It is through variations on this theme that most of us attempt to become the in-itself-for-itself, the pure subjectivity that will also be an object. But either I am an object for a subject, or that subject is an object for me; never both at once. Hence I can never succeed in my attempts to become the in-itself-for-itself; I cannot hope to become an object while simultaneously retaining the power to objectify.

The fact that I relate to other people either as a subject to an object or vice versa has one important implication. It implies that in the universe of *Being and Nothingness* two free subjects can never truly encounter each other. The for-itself is profoundly alone, for she can never share her world with another subject. Thus Sartre rejects Heidegger's claim, in *Being and Time*, that my fundamental relation with other people is *Mitsein* ('being-with'):

> It is therefore useless for human-reality to seek to get out of this dilemma: one must either transcend the Other or allow oneself to be transcended by him. The essence of the relations between consciousnesses is not the *Mitsein*; it is conflict. (BN, p. 429)

Or, as Sartre famously put it in his 1944 play *No Exit*, 'Hell is other people.'[10]

FURTHER READING

Sartre describes the being of the in-itself in the 'Introduction' to *Being and Nothingness*, then devotes the first chapter to 'The Origin of Negation' in the for-itself. Jospeh S. Catalano's *A Commentary on Jean-Paul Sartre's* 'Being and Nothingness' (Chicago: University of Chicago Press, 1980) is a helpful guide to these sections, as indeed to the entire work. Also useful is the chapter 'Being and Negation' in Peter Caws, *Sartre* (London: Routledge, 1984).

Sartre's conception of being-for-others has generated a large secondary literature. Gregory McCulloch's *Using Sartre* (London: Routledge, 1994) devotes a helpful chapter to the topic. Michael Theunissen's *The Other*, trans. Christopher MacCann (Cambridge, MA: MIT Press, 1984) is also useful, though rather more advanced.

For those who want to go deeper into Sartre's ontology, Hazel E. Barnes, 'Sartre's Ontology: The Revealing and Making of Being', in *The Cambridge Companion to Sartre*, ed. Christina Howells (Cambridge: Cambridge University Press, 1992) is useful. Paul Arthur Schilpp (ed.) *The Philosophy of Jean-Paul Sartre* (La Salle, ILL: Open Court, 1981) contains several relevant essays. Klaus Hartmann's *Sartre's Ontology: A Study of* Being and Nothingness *in the Light of Hegel's Logic* (Evanston, IL: Northwestern University Press, 1966) is difficult and intended for the advanced student of Sartre.

From ontology to anti-essentialism: Sartre's attack on human nature

We have now sketched, all too briefly, some of the technical apparatus used by Sartre and the basis of his ontology. However, it is not because of his contributions to these relatively obscure topics alone that Sartre occupies the place he does in twentieth-century philosophy. After all, neither ontological dualism nor intentionality are original contributions to philosophy, however novel Sartre's defence of them. Instead, Sartre's claim to philosophical originality and importance rests upon the conclusions he draws from these technical contributions, conclusions that, if true, are of the first importance for our moral and political thought. It is, therefore, to these conclusions that we now turn.

Existentialism and human nature

Sartre believes that his ontology and the thesis that consciousness is intentional both lead to the same conclusion: that the for-itself has no intrinsic nature. There is nothing it has to be; indeed, nothing it *can* be. Instead, it is up to it to define itself, to choose itself without constraints upon that choice. This radical and important thesis provides the basis for Sartre's ethical thought.

Let us explore this theme by way of an examination of Sartre's famous post-war lecture, 'Existentialism Is a

Humanism', for it is here that the thesis that the for-itself has no nature is most forcefully expounded. In this lecture, Sartre asks us to compare the for-itself to a mere thing, especially a manufactured object – his own example is a paper knife. Such things, Sartre says, have an essence, a nature. That is to say, there is something that they have to be, failing which they are inferior examples of that kind of thing. This is obviously the case with manufactured goods. A paper knife will be a good exemplar of the kind of thing it is just in so far as it has the qualities that enable it to fulfil those functions for which it was designed. It must be sharp, have an easily graspable handle, and so on. If it is beautifully made but so fragile that it would likely break if used, we would be forced to say that it was not a good paper knife (though perhaps it might be a good *ornament*).

Thus manufactured goods have a nature. Here, their nature functions as a *normative* concept; it provides us with a standard against which we can measure the thing. A knife is good just in so far as it is capable of fulfilling its function, and similarly for cups, chairs, watches and so on. Now, how does it come about that the paper knife has a nature? Sartre claims that such goods are provided with natures by us when we manufacture them. The paper knife is built *in order to* fulfil some function. That is what makes it a paper knife. Because the *concept* of the paper knife precedes its manufacture, both chronologically and causally, we can say of such goods that their *essence* precedes their *existence*. That is, before they existed as a particular entity, they were conceived; they were manufactured by someone who already had the idea of this kind of thing in mind, and who then produced it in accordance with this idea, bearing in mind what kind of thing they were producing, and what kind of function it was to serve. Since the idea of the paper knife *precedes* the manufacture of the individual implement, we can say:

> that its essence – that is to say the sum of the formulae and the quali-
> ties which made its production and its definition possible – precedes
> its existence. (EH, p. 348)

But, Sartre argues, with regard to the human being – the for-itself – the situation is quite different. That this is the case has been obscured, Sartre thinks, by a philosophy still too much in thrall to religious notions. In theistic thought, the human being is thought of as analogous to manufactured objects, since we too are held to be the product of a creator. God might have conceived of the kind of being he wanted us to be before he created us; if this were the case, then for us too our essence would precede our existence. But if God does not exist – and Sartre holds that there is no good reason to think otherwise – then we have no creator. We are, presumably, the chance creation of blind forces of nature, not the work of an intelligent designer. Since no one and nothing conceived of us before we were created,

> there is at least one being whose existence comes before its essence, a being which exists before it can be defined by any conception of it. That being is man. (EH, p. 349)

Sartre here offers us an independent argument for the conclusion he had already reached in *Being and Nothingness*: that the for-itself is a radically different kind of being from any mere thing, in that the for-itself is the kind of being whose being is perpetually in question. In *Being and Nothingness* Sartre had argued that it was the fact that we were separated from being, even from our own being, by a nothingness which placed our being in question for ourselves. Now he is suggesting that we do not have an essence because we were not created by a god.

Though the arguments are for similar conclusions, this second approach draws our attention to certain implications of Sartre's doctrine that otherwise might go unnoticed. To say that we are beings for whom our existence precedes our essence is to say that we are beings who have no *nature*. This is a thesis that has potentially far-reaching consequences. To see this, think of the ways in which the appeal to the nature of something functions in everyday language. For example, if someone is upset because his cat has killed a bird, we might say to him something like 'You can't blame the cat; hunting is in its nature.' What we would mean by this, I think, is that it would be inappropriate to blame the cat for its hunting, because it is something that it is not able to control or change. Nor can we hope to alter its behaviour; if hunting is in its nature, it is probably ineradicable. What is in something's nature is fixed – or at least cannot be easily altered – and is beyond blame or punishment (and equally beyond praise).

Very often, appeals to human nature function in an analogous way. Think, for example, of the common argument against socialism which appeals to human nature:

> Socialism is a very nice idea in theory, but it is completely impractical. It can't work because people just are naturally greedy and selfish. Therefore they will not willingly share their wealth with everyone else.

In this common kind of argument, the appeal to human nature alleges that facts about our essence function as constraints on what we can hope to achieve. Since it is in our nature to behave in certain ways – to be greedy, or to care more for people of the same skin colour as us than for those of a different skin colour, or to repress our sexual desires, or whatever – we have simply to accept these facts about ourselves and attempt to work around them.

On a more personal level, it is often held that each of us has an individual nature. This claim is perhaps most common these days with regard to sexuality. In the wake of Freud's work on the manner in which desire powerfully shapes the individual psyche, it is often said today that we each have a sexual nature. Some of us, for example, are homosexuals. This is a fact about our nature, which probably implies that if we attempt to ignore it or repress it we will be very unhappy. We might even suffer very serious mental illness. Since our sexuality is in each of our natures, we cannot hope to change it. Instead we must accommodate ourselves to this fact. (There is a conservative version of this line of thought, which denies that we each individually have a sexual nature but which holds, instead, that human beings as a species have such a nature, and that that nature is heterosexual. Thus, this line of thought concludes, homosexuality is unnatural.)

Sartre is denying that we have any such nature, either individually or as a species. Instead, he claims that is up to each of us to mould ourselves in the image we choose:

> What do we mean by saying that [for us] existence precedes essence? We mean that man first of all exists, encounters himself, surges up in

the world – and defines himself afterwards … Man is nothing else but that which he makes of himself. That is the first principle of existentialism. (EH, p. 349)

We shall shortly explore the consequences of the existentialist rejection of the idea of human nature in detail. Before we do so, however, it is worth pausing a moment to assess the arguments that Sartre presents for his contention that the for-itself has no nature.

Assessing the arguments

Sartre presents his argument against the idea that the for-itself has a nature in 'Existentialism Is a Humanism' as though it were an incontrovertible proof. It must be said that by itself it fails to establish this conclusion. Sartre is right to point out that we differ from manufactured objects in that we are not consciously created. But human beings might more profitably be compared to (other) animals than to manufactured objects. After all, if there is no God then animals and plants have come about in exactly the same way as have human beings: through the chance workings of blind forces. Thus for horses and fish and trees, too, existence precedes essence, in the sense that no one *conceived* of them before they came into being. Yet surely it is very implausible to say of them what Sartre says of human beings: that they have no nature, and that therefore it is up to each of them to make themselves the kind of beings they wish to be. After all, it seems very plausible to say, as we did earlier, that hunting is in a cat's nature. In general, we may say, animals have a nature if anything does. Bees must live out their lives in their hives if they are to flourish, and play out the roles within the hives for which their nature equips them. Thus it is completely out of place to accuse the queen bee of authoritarianism, for example, or praise the worker for industriousness. Such notions of praise and blame are appropriate only with regard to beings who can reflect upon their roles and form the project of changing them.

If this is the case, then the fact that human beings have evolved as a result of chance, without anyone or anything conceiving of them beforehand, will not be sufficient to establish the contention that the for-itself has no nature. I think, therefore, that this argument fails. However, it is not, for all that, necessarily worthless. It remains of some value in so far as it highlights an important implication of the thesis that the for-itself is fundamentally free. We are not simply free in the sense that we can make choices about how to live; we are free in the far more radical sense that our choices are not constrained by a pre-existing nature.

Perhaps we ought not to be overly critical of Sartre's argument in 'Existentialism Is a Humanism'. The latter was, after all, a popular lecture, not a philosophical treatise. Perhaps, then, we ought to forgive Sartre for relying upon arguments that are more suggestive than conclusive. At least, we may do so if Sartre has elsewhere been able to offer better arguments for the contention that the for-itself has no nature. Sartre does indeed believe that he has established this, in *Being and Nothingness*.

What must ultimately bear the weight of Sartre's argument is precisely the technical apparatus that we sketched in the preceding chapters. Two elements of that apparatus are essential here. First is the contention that the for-itself is the being by whom nothingness comes to the world, that the for-itself is to itself its own nothingness. Second is Sartre's appropriation of the Husserlian idea that consciousness is always consciousness of something that is outside itself; that is, that it is intentional. For Sartre, both of these claims point in the same direction as the argument he presents in 'Existentialism Is a Humanism'; that is, they help establish that the for-itself has no nature. Let us examine the relation of each of these claims to that thesis in turn.

To say that the for-itself is the being by whom nothingness comes to the world is, as we have seen, to say that the for-itself is separated from all causal chains by a nothingness. Thus a nothingness intervenes between the for-itself and its past, between the for-itself and its environment, even between the for-itself and itself. But this is nothing more than to say that the for-itself has no nature. After all, what could such a nature be other than some kind of causal power? Think, for example, of the human nature argument in one of its currently most widespread forms: the sociobiological thesis that as a species we have a nature, which has been determined by the course of evolution. Sociobiologists claim, for example, that we have gendered natures; that human males are naturally sexually promiscuous whereas human females naturally seek stable relationships with a single partner. The claim that is being made here is not just that it is in our interests to cultivate these contrasting kinds of relationships (because males will be able to pass on their genes more effectively if they have multiple partners, whereas females, who quite literally are left holding the baby, will require assistance to bring up their offspring), but that we are unconsciously motivated to engage in the corresponding kinds of behaviour. Thus males are naturally Cassanovas, females naturally faithful; whether or not they have ever heard of the selfish gene.

But this is precisely what Sartre denies. Between our genes, which the sociobiologist takes to be exerting a causal power on our behaviour, and our consciousness (which, Sartre holds, is responsible for all our behaviour) a nothingness intervenes. Animals may well be determined by their genes; the sociobiological story is probably true with regard to them. But the for-itself is never determined by anything; not by its genes, not by its environment and not by its history.

An exactly parallel point can be established via an examination of Sartre's second claim, that consciousness is intentional, if indeed Sartre is right in holding that the corollary of this thesis is that consciousness is empty. Whereas the fact that a nothingness separates the for-itself from all causal powers prevents it from being determined from without, by mechanical (or biomechanical) forces, the fact that consciousness is necessarily empty prevents it from being determined from within, by psychic forces.

This follows, Sartre believes, from the notion of intentionality. Since consciousness is intentional, it never incorporates anything into itself. Since it must remain blank in order to reflect the world accurately, whatever it now mirrors is snatched away from it, without trace or remainder. This is the case, not only with regard to what the for-itself perceives outside of itself, but equally with regard to whatever emotions or dispositions might temporarily characterize it. Since emotions, for example, cannot be things – since things cannot enter consciousness – their being must be intentional.

Hence, they too must dissipate as soon as the consciousness that intends them ceases to maintain them in being. Thus, the for-itself can be melancholy, or cheerful, or pensive, only so long as it intends itself as having these characteristics. Hence emotions can exist 'only as immediate self-consciousness':

> Pleasure can not be distinguished – even logically – from conscious-ness of pleasure. Consciousness (of) pleasure is constitutive of the pleasure as the very mode of its existence, as the material of which it is made. (BN, p. xxx)

The implications Sartre draws from this thesis are quite radical, but in some ways the thesis itself is intuitive. Sartre is claiming that there is no difference between experiencing pleasure and being conscious of experiencing pleasure. This much, at least, seems very plausible. What would it mean to say of someone that they were experiencing pleasure but they didn't know it? Or that they were experiencing pain without being aware of it? Surely feelings exist only so long as they are consciously felt – that is what makes them feelings.

Sartre claims that these feelings exist only so long as we intend them, because there can never be any*thing* in consciousness. There cannot be a little nucleus that *is* pleasure, or contentment, or boredom, and that would determine consciousness as pleased, or bored, and so on. This is brought out nicely by Sartre's description of suffering. Since the suffering person can never *be* their suffering, but must instead sustain it in being by a choice of themselves as suffering, they suffer, and at they same time they suffer 'from not suffering enough':

> What we call 'noble' or 'good' or 'true' suffering and what moves us is the suffering which we read on the faces of others, better yet in portraits, in the face of a statue, in a tragic mask. It is a suffering which has *being* ... which overflows the consciousness which we have of it; it is there in the midst of the world, impenetrable, and dense, like this tree or this stone; it endures; finally it is what it is. (BN, p. 91)

This is suffering as ideal or as norm, suffering as the sufferer would like to experience it. It would be something that comes to them from without, takes hold of them without their consent and over which they have neither say nor control. Given that consciousness is intentional, however, this suffering in-itself is in fact never experienced. Instead,

> The suffering which I experience … is never adequate suffering, due to the fact that it nihilates itself as in itself by the very act by which it founds itself. It escapes as suffering toward the consciousness of suffering. I can never be *surprised* by it, for it *is* only to the exact degree that I experience it. (BN, p. 92)

The contents of consciousness exist only to the extent that I intend them. Thus there is never anything in my consciousness except what I have, in some sense, consented to.

Since nothing can be in consciousness except what I intend, there can be no intrapsychic determinism. Since I cannot *be* suffering, I suffer only to the extent that I allow myself to suffer. I am not, therefore, made to suffer by forces beyond my control. At the level of consciousness, I can never be moulded, shaped, pulled in one direction or another by forces over which I have no control, whether these forces come from without or within me.[11]

Thus the for-itself is always free to make of itself what it will. No force can determine it without its consent. A nothingness intervenes to prevent such forces *causing* it to be this or that. But we can go further still. It is not only that consciousness cannot be determined by forces, whether interior or exterior to itself, because a nothingness always drains such forces of any causal powers over such consciousness. Consciousness is not only never determined to be this or that by such forces. Consciousness is simply unable to *be* anything; hence, not only is the for-itself free to form itself as it wishes, without external constraint, it cannot impose *internal* constraints on itself. If it were able to impose such constraints on itself, it would no longer be a for-itself. It would possess stable characteristics, it would be fixed – in other words, it would be in-itself.

Consequences of anti-essentialism

What does Sartre mean by saying that the for-itself can never *be* anything? We can best understand Sartre's position here by reference once more to 'Existentialism Is a Humanism'. There, as we saw, Sartre argues that the for-itself is the being that is characterized by the fact that for it, and for it alone, existence precedes essence. The for-itself *is* before it is anything in particular. Thus the for-itself exists without essence or nature, without there being anything that would function for it as a normative ideal to which it must live up. This position has two implications, which are slightly in tension with each other:

1. Since we do not have a nature or an essence, it is up to each of us to make ourselves the kind of being we wish to be. We each have the project of creating ourselves.
2. Nevertheless, there is a sense in which this is a project that has to fail. We are each free to attempt to make ourselves however we wish, but we always necessarily fail to *be* anything at all.

Let us now explore these implications in a little more detail.

We have seen that, since we do not have an essence and since forces, both interior and exterior, are powerless to determine consciousness, the for-itself is always free to make itself as it wishes. Now, although the route that Sartre takes to this conclusion is unique, the position itself is far from unprecedented. We could, in fact, see Sartre as laying down ontological foundations for a rather standard version of liberalism – the doctrine that individuals are able, and ought be allowed, to reflect upon and either endorse or reject the values and norms of their society and their culture.[12] Sartre stands opposed to all those forces, and all those political philosophies, that liberalism opposes – to the claim that we ought to respect traditional ways of life, institutions and practices merely because they are traditional, to those political thinkers who hold that too much individual liberty is corrosive of social order, to those who hold that we are constituted by values and norms we simply inherit from our past.

But although a liberal might agree with Sartre that our power to question received values and practices, and the freedom that this power entails, could be described – perhaps a little hyperbolically – by way of his dictum that existence precedes essence, the liberal is not normally committed to the second part of Sartre's doctrine of consciousness. The liberal, that is, might hold that our attempt to make ourselves in the image we choose might be wholly successful. Once our project is complete, we may be able to say of ourselves that we *are* what we have set out to become.

An example might make this clearer. Perhaps, as a result of embracing liberalism, I set myself the project of freeing myself from a religious upbringing I now regard as repressive and narrow-minded, and recreating myself as a tolerant cosmopolitan who is beyond such parochial loyalties. Let us assume that I am successful in this project.[13] Now, according to the liberal there is no reason for me not to identify myself with my project. I may now say of myself that I *am* a tolerant, open-minded cosmopolitan. Sartre, on the other hand, denies me the right to claim this. For him, human existence does not just *precede* essence; it is exclusive of it. So long as I am a for-itself, I cannot say that I *am* anything at all. Since nothing can ever inhabit consciousness – 'There is no inertia in consciousness' (BN, p. 61) – it is not only at the start that I am not anything; it is always, so long as I exist. To that extent, there is a sense in which my project to create myself as this or that must necessarily fail.

We are now at the very heart of Sartre's doctrine of the for-itself, and it is worth lingering here a while the better to appreciate the force of Sartre's position. I will explore its implications – implications that, as we shall see, are at once practical and philosophical – by way of examining two of Sartre's own vivid examples.

The gambler

The first example concerns a well-known problem in philosophy, the problem of explaining weakness of the will. What is going on when I find myself breaking my resolution not to smoke, for example, or when I find myself tempted to eat that second piece of chocolate cake in spite of my sincere desire to lose weight? The example Sartre sketches concerns an inveterate gambler, who has, however, made the decision no longer to gamble. Now, as he approaches the gaming table, he 'suddenly sees all his resolutions melt away' (BN, p. 32) and he finds himself tempted to gamble once more. What is happening to the gambler in such a case and how ought we to describe it?

Philosophers have sometimes explained this kind of case by postulating the existence of forces that, if we do not carefully guard against them, threaten to seize us and pull us in directions we may not wish to go. Instinctual drives, or blind passions, may cause us to act against our better judgement. Sartre denies that such forces can ever cause us to act in any way, of course, and this route is therefore denied to him. Instead, he explains the phenomenon of weakness of the will by reference to his doctrine that nothing can inhabit consciousness. The gambler has assessed his behaviour, seen that it threatened him with financial ruin, and renounced it. But in order to guarantee that he would not change his mind in the heat of the moment, he has attempted to place something inside consciousness. He attempts to set up his resolution as a barrier, an external power that will secure him against temptation. It will, he hopes, act as a kind of guardrail, preventing him from gambling. It will provide an obstacle that his freedom cannot cross.

But now, when the opportunity to gamble presents itself, the gambler sees that all his efforts have been in vain. He has not succeeded in the slightest in setting up his resolution as a barrier against his freedom. Sartre imagines him speaking thus:

> It seemed to me that I had established a *real barrier* between gambling and myself, and now I suddenly perceive that my former understanding of the situation is no more than a memory of an idea, a memory of a feeling ... After having patiently built up barriers and walls, after enclosing myself in the magic circle of a resolution, I perceive with anguish that *nothing* prevents me from gambling. (BN, p. 33)

Nothing can inhabit consciousness, not a force, not a mechanism and certainly not a resolution. In order for my resolution not to smoke, not to overeat or not to gamble to be effective, I need to remake it every time the opportunity to relapse presents itself. That I spent all of yesterday swearing I had renounced gambling for good will not help me now. Nor would having resisted the temptation one thousand times before come to my aid. Each time I must start afresh; each time I must decide anew whether or not I will gamble.

The homosexual

The example of the gambler concerns an everyday situation: someone attempting to erect a barrier at the heart of their own consciousness. That they would seek to do this is perfectly comprehensible: we have all experienced the powerlessness of our resolutions in the face of temptation. The example of the homosexual concerns a phenomenon that is no less commonplace, yet which has received extraordinarily little philosophical attention. It concerns someone identifying himself or herself with their sexuality.[14]

There is no doubt that the phenomenon this example points to is real enough. Many gay people strongly identify themselves with their sexuality. They are not, say, French, black, a doctor and *in addition* gay; instead they are *essentially* gay. Gayness is a constitutive ingredient in their identity.

This is, moreover, merely one example of a phenomenon that is much more general. Ask yourself how you would answer the question 'who are you?' when this question does not ask for your name, but instead asks you to define what makes you the kind of person that you are. We might usefully think of this kind of question in terms of a distinction philosophers make, between the 'accidental' and the 'essential' properties of an entity. The essential properties of an object, for example, are those properties which make it the kind of thing it is. A knife, for example, necessarily has a blade, and in the absence of a blade it simply wouldn't be a knife. The accidental properties of an object, on the other hand, are those properties which it could conceivably lose without ceasing to be the kind of thing it is. The colour of an object would be an accidental property, for example: a knife remains a knife, no matter what colour it is.

Applying this distinction to the case in hand, when someone asks you who you are, she may be thought to be asking you to list your essential properties: to identify those aspects of yourself that make you the person you are and in the absence of which you would not be the same person. You probably wouldn't answer this question by saying that you are a hamburger eater. No matter how much you might love hamburgers, you probably do not think that this taste is constitutive of your identity. You might, however, answer the question by mentioning your religion or your nationality, saying, 'I am a Muslim' or 'I am British.' Perhaps you might mention your family: 'I am a father' is a comprehensible response to the question. Very frequently, at least in modern Western countries, people refer to their career or profession in answering this kind of question (one of Sartre's examples in *Being and Nothingness* concerns a man who identifies himself with being a waiter).

But the tendency to identify ourselves in terms of our sexuality is, in the wake of Freud, especially strong. This would seem to be an essential property of our identities, if anything is. Think of your own case: wouldn't an alteration in your sexual orientation (whether from homosexual to heterosexual or vice versa) be one of the most significant alterations you could undergo – an alteration so significant that there might be some sense in which you would no longer be the same person?

If this is the case, then it seems to be sensible to claim that you *are* homosexual (or heterosexual); that your sexuality is part of your being. Sartre will deny that it is legitimate for you to say this. You are a human being; that is, a being that does not have an essence at all. Nothing causally determines your behaviour; nor is there any normative ideal to which you must conform. You cannot *be* anything at all.[15]

You will remember that the guiding thread Sartre followed in elucidating the being of the for-itself was the question. The for-itself was the being who was able to question, able to distance itself from being in order to question it. Sartre examined the conditions of possibility of the question, and concluded that the for-itself must be beyond causal determination; the being that is beyond being. Now he will forge an even closer relation between the question and the for-itself. Since the for-itself is the being for whom its existence precedes its essence – it *is* before it is this or that – the for-itself is the being that has to forge its own being. What it will be is up to it, a project for it to carry out. Put another way, the for-itself is, for itself, always in question: 'The for-itself is a being such that in its being, its being is in question' (BN, p. 174; cf. pp. 23, 29, 540).

The temporality of the for-itself

We have seen that the for-itself is a being whose being is always in question for itself, upon whom causality cannot act, which can never *be* anything. Sartre sums up these qualities in a formula that is as striking as it is paradoxical. In contrast to the in-itself, which 'is what it is' (BN, p. xlii), the for-itself can be defined 'as being what is not and not being what it is' (BN, p. xli).

It is the love for this kind of paradoxical assertion that many Anglophone philosophers find so infuriating in Continental philosophers. They point out that this aphorism is, strictly speaking, a simple contradiction. Nothing can be what it is not; nor fail to be what it is. What can Sartre mean by this contradictory assertion?

Actually, Sartre has ample warrant for his aphorism. If the for-itself is the being whose being is perpetually in question, if a nothingness always intervenes between it and all forces that might determine it, then there is a clear sense in which we can say that it is not what it is. To some extent, we clearly can say that someone *is* a gambler, or a homosexual (or a waiter, or a Greek, or a lesbian and so forth). Though Sartre might be right, that in a deep sense the for-itself can never be anything, we cannot do without this shallower sense of being, which we draw upon when we make this kind of statement. Our language and our conceptual resources would be impoverished without it; moreover, our everyday life seems to require this shallow sense of being (think of the difficulties that would arise if we could never describe someone as a doctor or a police officer). Moreover, facts about persons give us philosophical justifications for these descriptive terms. We can, for example, ascribe character traits to people. For example, statements such as 'Sam is irascible' or 'Jane is cunning' can be unproblematically true or false, depending on the characteristic behaviour of the people mentioned. Nevertheless, though there may be ample warrant for making such statements, it remains true that, in a deeper sense, the for-itself cannot be *anything*. What this means in practice is that, though it is unproblematic to describe someone as having this or that character trait, we must not be misled into thinking that having this character trait is an unvarying or unalterable fact about that person. An irascible person can be relaxed and easygoing upon occasions; the fact of her irascibility does not determine her behaviour. Indeed, she can even cease to be irascible and become easygoing. Since she is not, in a deep sense, anything at all, her character traits are always open to change.

Thus we can make sense of half of Sartre's aphorism, the half that states that the for-itself is not what it is. As we have seen, this means that it is not (in the deep sense of 'being') what it is (in the shallow sense). In our example, Sam is irascible, which is to say that he displays the character traits typically so described, and is not irascible, which is to say that it is always up to him whether these character traits will be expressed on a particular occasion, or whether in fact he will continue to have these traits at all.

What of the other half of Sartre's formula, however? Can we make sense of that? We have seen what justifies Sartre in saying that the for-itself is not what it is, but what warrants the assertion that it *is* what it *is not*? The clearest way to make sense of this statement, I think, is by reference to Sartre's theory of temporality. For Sartre, the for-itself is essentially temporal; it exists only as a being in time. We have already seen, for instance, that the for-itself is never determined by its past. The fact that it has been this or that – irascible, for instance, or gay – does not imply that it must continue to be so. But the for-itself can differ from its past only if it is essentially in time; if, in fact, it exists as temporalization. The for-itself is the being who separates itself from itself by secreting nothingness, thus consigning what it is to its past. To put it another way, by temporalizing itself the for-itself brings temporality into being.

Thus, I am always separated from what I have been by a nothingness, which is nothing other than time itself. I am not my past. But my past is, nevertheless, an ineradicable aspect of my being. I can legitimately be said to be something (irascible, or gay) only to the extent that my past behaviour justifies the ascription:

> whatever I can be said to *be* in the sense of being-in-itself with full, compact density (he is quick-tempered, he is a civil servant, he is dissatisfied) is always *my past*. It is in the past that I am what I am. (BN, pp. 117–18)

This gives us another way of making sense of the first half of Sartre's aphorism. I am not what I am, in the sense that I am and yet am not my past. Sam is irascible to the extent that the disposition he has exhibited to irritability in the past justifies us in so describing him; he is, however, not irascible in that it depends upon his choice of himself whether he will continue to exhibit this disposition. In so far as I am anything, it is because I have been it. Sartre often quotes Hegel's dictum: *Wesen ist gewesen ist* – 'essence is what has been'.

How does Sartre's notion of temporality illuminate the other half of his formula? In what sense will it permit us to say that the for-itself is what it is not? We have seen that the for-itself is not what it is because it temporalizes itself; it separates itself from what it is by making it past. But to say that the for-itself separates itself from its past is at the same time to say that it projects itself towards its future – towards what it will be. The for-itself, as project towards … is *already* what it is *not yet*. Thus Sartre describes himself cautiously edging along a narrow mountain ledge. As he does so, he projects himself forwards in time, to the person he will be when he turns the corner and regains safer ground:

> I am indeed already there in the future; it is for the sake of that being which I will be there at the turning of the path that I now exert all my strength, and in this sense there is already a relation between my future being and my present being. But a nothingness has slipped into the heart of this relation; I *am* not the self which I will be. First I am not that self because time separates me from it. Secondly, I am not that self because what I am is not the foundation of what I will be. Finally I am not that self because no actual existent can determine strictly what I am going to be. Yet as I am already what I will be (otherwise I would not be interested in any one being more than another), *I am the self which I will be in the mode of not being it*. (BN, pp. 31–2)

Thus Sartre is and is not the self he will be. In some sense, he is already the person he is not yet; he is what he is not.

FURTHER READING

Attempts to define a human nature have a long history. Sartre's anti-essen-
tialist argument employs some of the same considerations Aristotle
utilized to opposite ends in his *Nichomachean Ethics* (many editions),
Book I.

Today, supporters of the view that human beings have a nature in some
substantive sense tend to rely on the work of sociobiologists. The classic
work in this context is Richard Dawkins, *The Selfish Gene* (Oxford: Oxford
University Press, 1976). E.O. Wilson's *On Human Nature* (Cambridge, MA:
Harvard University Press, 1978) has also been influential. Peter Singer
summarizes the conclusions of the sociobiologists and attempts to draw
the consequences of their thesis for political thought, all in around sixty
pages, in his *A Darwinian Left: Politics, Evolution and Cooperation*
(London: Weidenfeld & Nicolson, 1999). Singer accuses those who deny
that there is a human nature from which we can draw normative consequences of ignoring the scientific evidence; for the contrary position, put
by scientists, see R.C. Lewontin, Steven Rose and Leon J. Kamin, *Not in Our
Genes: Biology, Ideology, and Human Nature* (New York, Pantheon, 1984).
For an overview of the 'gay gene' debate, see Richard Horton, 'Is
Homosexuality Inherited?', *New York Review of Books*, July 1995.

I have argued that Sartre's position can profitably be compared with
mainstream liberal philosophy. For a good brief discussion of the liberal
tradition, see John Gray, *Liberalism*, 2nd edn (Buckingham: Open
University Press, 1995). Liberalism's strongest challenge today comes from
so-called 'communitarian' philosophers, who hold that our values are
constitutive of who we are and therefore cannot all coherently be ques-
tioned. It would seem that Sartre's thought is vulnerable to a similar line of
attack. For the communitarian critique of liberalism, see Daniel Bell,
Communitarianism and Its Critics (Oxford: Oxford University Press, 1993).

Weakness of the will is a perennial philosophical problem. Plato
attempts an explanation in the *Republic*, Aristotle in the *Nichomachean
Ethics*. A good contemporary overview of the topic is Justin Gosling's
Weakness of the Will (London: Routledge, 1990).

From ontology to ethics

Being and Nothingness advertises itself as an essay on ontology, and indeed it is largely taken up with ontological questions. Nevertheless, Sartre is little interested in ontology for its own sake. For him, the point of elaborating an ontology seems to be to delineate the being of the for-itself. It is this being which captures his attention. Centrally, Sartre is concerned with the problem of how we ought to live.

This is not, however, to say that Sartre's ontology is a mere prelude to his real subject, a disposable means of defining human being which can then safely be put aside. Instead, Sartre's central and original claim is that the ontology of the for-itself lays down the parameters for the answer to ethical questions.

The ethics of authenticity

For the past two centuries, moral philosophy has been dominated by debates between two broad positions. On the one side, there have been those thinkers who argue that certain kinds of acts are intrinsically right or wrong. Knowing this fact is sufficient to guide us. If, for example, I know that X is a charitable act, I ought (other things being equal) to do X. On the other hand, if I know that Y is an act of betrayal, I ought to refrain from doing Y. This position is known as 'deontology', from the Greek word for 'duty'. Deontologists argue that I ought to perform those actions which are my duty, and refrain from those which I have a duty not to perform. It is by focusing on the intrinsic character of the act that I ought to be guided.

Opposition to this position has come largely from those philosophers who call themselves 'consequentialists'. As the name implies, consequentialists argue that we ought to decide how to act by reference to the consequences of the various courses of actions open to us. From these alternatives I ought to select that act which has the best consequences (usually measured in terms of the amount of happiness produced by the act, or the number of preferences satisfied by it).

Very often, consequentialists and deontologists agree about *what* we should do, even if they disagree about *why* we should do it. Very often, that is, those actions which deontologists hold are our duty are also those actions which maximize preference-satisfaction or happiness. But sometimes the two come decisively apart. Deontologists might advocate actions that have worse consequences than other actions open to us, and consequentialists sometimes argue for courses of action that deontologists regard as simply immoral.

I want to demonstrate the extent to which the theoretical dispute between consequentialists and deontologists can become a practical disagreement, with an example that goes back to the early days of this dispute. In order to sketch my example, however, I will need to provide a little background.

Immanuel Kant (1724–1804) was one of the first, and remains perhaps the greatest, of the deontologists. He argued that reason alone was sufficient to guide our moral choices. From reason alone we can deduce what Kant called the 'categorical imperative', the fundamental law of Kant's ethics. In its best-known formulation, it states,

> Act only on that maxim by which you can at the same time will that it should become a universal law.

What this means, roughly, is that the test for whether an action is permissible or impermissible is whether it could be *universalized*.

We are permitted to perform only such actions that we could rationally will ought to become a law governing the actions of everyone. Thus Kant argues that the categorical imperative rules out lying. In order for me to lie successfully, it is necessary that most people tell the truth most of the time. If everyone lied all the time – or even if the percentage of lies crossed a certain threshold – no one would believe anything anyone said, and it would be impossible to lie (I cannot successfully lie to you unless you are convinced that I am telling you the truth). Therefore, lying is not the kind of thing that can be consistently universalized. For Kant, this is sufficient evidence that lying is wrong.

Consequentialists will in general support the conclusion that lying is wrong. Their reasons for this conclusion will, however, be very different from Kant's. Rather than holding that lying is always and necessarily wrong, consequentialists will, in order to support their contention, point to the results of lying. Now, holding that lying will, in general, have negative consequences (will lead to a decrease in happiness, or reduce the number of satisfied preferences) is consistent with holding that lying might be the right thing to do in particular circumstances. On this question, a deontologist and a consequentialist can be implacably opposed.

It was on just this question that Benjamin Constant, a French novelist and political thinker, attacked Kant. Whatever value truth-telling might usually possess, Constant argues, it cannot be the case that we have a duty to tell the truth at all times and in all circumstances. Consider the following case:

> A friend of yours rushes to your door, begging you to hide her. She tells you she is being chased by a psychotic murderer who wants to kill her. Sure enough, a few minutes later a man swinging an axe barges into your house and asks if you have seen your friend. Surely in these circumstances you ought to lie? The consequences of your lying (your friend escaping a horrible death) are clearly better than the consequences of your telling the truth, even if it is the case that lying is wrong in itself.

Kant was not swayed by this appeal to consequences. Even in this case, he held, we have a duty to tell the truth. If we have done our duty, he argues, we are not responsible for the consequences that might follow. If I tell the murderer the truth, and he catches and kills my friend, then it is he who is guilty of murder. But if I lie, then I take on responsibility for the consequences. Thus, if I attempt to deceive the murderer, telling him my friend has run off, and if, unbeknown to me, she actually has run off, as a result of my lie the murderer might catch her. In these circumstances, Kant holds, I might justly be accused of being the cause of her death.

We can be sure that Constant would remain unconvinced by this argument. Thus it can happen that deontologists advocate actions that consequentialists find morally unacceptable. More commonly, however, the boot is on the other foot; it is the consequentialist who stands accused of supporting actions that are objectionable. Deontologists are fond of pointing out that circumstances can arise in which the consequentialist will be committed to a course of action which seems counter-intuitive. One famous example runs as follows:

> Imagine you are the sheriff of a small town in the American South. A white woman in the town has been raped by a black man. You don't know who the perpetrator is, nor do you have any evidence which will help you to track him down quickly. You know, however, that if you do not hang someone for the crime soon, the white population of the town will form a lynch mob, which will certainly kill many innocent blacks. You have in your custody a black man, who has been held overnight for a minor offence. Since he was in jail at the time of the rape, you know that he is not guilty of the crime. But you also know that no one else knows that he is innocent.

As a good consequentialist, you reason as follows: if no one is hanged for this crime, many people will die. If, on the other hand, I frame this innocent man, these deaths will be prevented. Naturally, the suffering of this man is to be regretted (the more so since I know him to be innocent). However, since the consequences of framing and hanging him are clearly better than the consequences of not doing so, I ought to frame him.

Thus the dispute between deontologists and consequentialists is not just a theoretical debate. It can also be a sharp disagreement about what ought to be done, a disagreement upon which questions of life and death may turn.

I do not wish to try to assess the rights and wrongs of this disagreement, to try to see whether the balance of reason lies with the consequentialists or with the deontologists (or whether some middle course can be struck between them). Instead, I want to examine Sartre's radical alternative to both consequentialism and deontology, an alternative that focuses on entirely different entities as the locus of moral assessment.

So far I have focused on what sets deontologists and consequentialists apart. We might instead concentrate on what they share. Though they differ on how to assess actions, they agree that it is actions upon which we should direct our attention in looking for what it is that constitutes moral worth. This might seem simply obvious; morality is concerned with right and wrong, and it is actions which are right and wrong. But there is an alternative way to approach ethics in general. Rather than focus upon *actions*, we could assess the *agents* who perform them.

Focusing upon agents and not actions is not itself an original approach. Agent-centred ethics goes back at least to the ancient Greeks. Greek thinkers like Aristotle argued that we should focus on the character of actors, rather than the actions they perform. This approach, known as 'virtue ethics', assesses the morality of particular actions only derivatively: the right action is that which would be performed by a virtuous person.

But though Sartre's general approach to ethics is not unprecedented, in so far as there have been previous ethical theories that advocated an agent or character centred assessment of moral worth, nevertheless Sartre's position is crucially different from these older approaches. The virtue ethicists advocated the cultivation of those qualities of the person which were widely regarded as virtues (whether they in fact justified these virtues by reference to some universally binding conception of human nature, as Aristotle did, or whether they held that the fact that their society valued these qualities was all the justification needed). Thus Aristotle advocated the cultivation of moderation, justice, courage and so on – qualities that he regarded as characteristic of the good person. In China at about the same time, Confucius, working in a different but still recognizably a virtue tradition, had a correspondingly different list – he seems to have thought that the most important virtues were loyalty, trust, generosity, modesty and courtesy. Nevertheless, though there is room for a disagreement about precisely which character traits are the virtues we ought to inculcate in ourselves, virtue ethicists all propose a more or less lengthy list of character traits that are commonly held to be moral traits. On both of these scores, Sartre veers decisively away from the virtue ethics traditions.

A little thought will show that Sartre cannot accept any of these lists as his own. What could ground any of the virtues? There appear to be two major kinds of justifications to which we might appeal in arguing for this or that virtue. The first such justification, the one to which Aristotle appealed in developing his ethics, is the alleged nature of the human being. In his *Nichomachean Ethics*, Aristotle utilizes precisely the same kinds of considerations to which Sartre will appeal 2500 years later, to argue for a diametrically opposed conclusion. Aristotle notes that in general we can establish the good of a thing – its *telos*, or the end it ought to fulfil – by appeal to its function. Thus we can say that, since a knife is an instrument that has the function of cutting, a good knife is a knife that has qualities that enable it to fulfil that function. By a good or a *telos*, Aristotle clearly means a nature, in the sense of a normative manner of being by reference to which we can assess the worth of something. It is, therefore, in direct opposition to a theory like Sartre's which denies the existence of *human* nature that Aristotle makes his next move. He argues that human beings have a function, and therefore a *telos*.

What is that *telos* and how does Aristotle deduce its content? Aristotle argues that the function of a thing will be that capacity it is able to fulfil better than anything else can. A shoe can be utilized as a hammer; so can a rock. Nevertheless, their function is clearly not hammering on this criterion, since neither of them fulfils that function as well as does a hammer. Thus, in general, if we want to deduce the *telos* of human beings, we must locate that function that they fulfil better than anything else.

This style of argument encourages Aristotle to seek the good for human beings in those abilities that differentiate us from other animals. Unsurprisingly, given this approach, Aristotle finds that our good is to be identified with the exercise of our rationality. The virtues, then, will be those traits of character which will enable us to pursue this good.

Sartre never explicitly replies to this argument, though the close parallel between it and the argument of 'Existentialism Is a Humanism' suggests that he had it in mind when he wrote that lecture. I imagine, though, that his reply might go something like the following.

Why suppose that the good life for us must consist in the exercise of a function that is unique to us? Supposing that it does presuppose that the universe is so ordered that everything will have its appointed function and there will be no overlap in functions. But why should that be the case, unless the universe was designed by a creator? Aristotle might be supposing that the universe was in fact designed by a creator, but he presents no credible evidence for this conclusion. In the absence of evidence for such a creator, we have no reason to think that Aristotle has identified the good life correctly – or indeed to think that there is such a good life that is normatively binding on human beings.

The other route to a defence of the virtues is conventionalist. We might hold that we ought to cultivate the virtues because we are the kind of beings we are in virtue of a certain kind of upbringing. Given our society, with its norms, conventions and practices, we will identify with these virtues and be motivated to act upon them.

How might Sartre reply to this line of argument? He would, I think, deny its premise. It is not the case that we are the kinds of beings we are in virtue of our upbringing. Neither a universal nature nor a local environment can cause the behaviour, the emotions or the character of a for-itself. The for-itself is so constituted that a nothingness intervenes between it and all such supposedly causal forces. It is up to me to accept my culture's values, or to reject them – and the fact that they are my culture's values does not in itself give me any reason (or excuse) for exempting them from critical evaluation. As we shall see, people commonly seek excuses for attempting to refuse the heavy burden of freedom. Both justifications we have examined – that the virtues are grounded in the

natural constitution of human beings and that the virtues are justified simply by the fact that they are characteristic of a particular
society – are, in Sartre's eyes, no more than such excuses.

Thus, rather than attempt to ground his virtues by reference to
such philosophical justifications, Sartre holds that it is always up to
each of us to choose the manner in which we shall live. This is not to
say, however, that Sartre simply gives up the task of moral assessment, or that he has no resources for judging between the choices of
individuals. The very fact that it is up to each of us to choose our
values, what constitutes a virtue for us and what a reason for action
itself gives Sartre a means of assessment of these choices. To the
extent that we willingly and deliberately assume the burden of
choice which this places on us, our choice will be *authentic*.

In other words, Sartre's virtue ethics contains but a single value.
We are all to cultivate the virtue of authenticity in ourselves, where
'authenticity' means the acceptance of our place in the cosmos, of
the fact that we are each alone, without excuse or reason for being,
abandoned to choose our values without reference to anything that
could justify them in the eyes of the universe. Authenticity means
accepting our burden of radical freedom, the fact that values are
not, as Sartre says, inscribed in an 'intelligible heaven' (EH, p. 353),
and that therefore we must create them ourselves. Inauthenticity,
the one vice on the Sartrean view, will therefore consist in the opposite – the attempt to find an excuse for our actions, a reason why we
had to act that way (I couldn't help it; it was my parents; my environment; I wasn't responsible for my actions; *or*, on the other hand,
my action was uniquely right; it was in accordance with the will of
God or with human nature; rationality dictated that I had to act that
way).

Sartre's ethics of authenticity is perhaps at its clearest in
'Existentialism Is a Humanism'. Let us, therefore, examine the argument of that lecture in some detail.

Sartre develops his ethics by way of a famous example, the case
of a pupil of his who came to him for advice during the war (at a
time when France was occupied by the German army). This young
man was torn between two mutually exclusive courses of action. On
the one hand he desired to go to Britain to join the Free French

Forces (FFF). If he took this course of action, he might be able to fight for the liberty of France and avenge the death of his older brother, killed in the German offensive of 1940. On the other hand, he could stay with his mother, who was living apart from his collaborationist father and who was still deeply in mourning for his brother. He knew that his going would plunge his mother into despair. He also knew that if he set out for Britain he might find himself stuck indefinitely in Spain or he might find himself consigned to office duty for the FFF.

> Consequently, he found himself confronted by two very different modes of action; the one concrete, immediate, but directed towards only one individual; and the other an action addressed to an end infinitely greater, a national collectivity, but for that very reason ambiguous – and it might be frustrated on the way. At the same time, he was hesitating between two kinds of morality; on the one side the morality of sympathy, of personal devotion and, on the other side, a morality of wider scope but of more debatable validity. He had to choose between those two. (EH, p. 354)

Sartre then throws down the challenge to more traditional moral systems: resolve this young man's dilemma in a manner that is rationally justified.

Sartre himself examines and assesses two responses to the dilemma, the first Christian, the second Kantian. We can also deduce a response to the consequentialist from what he says. I will therefore examine each of these in turn.

What does Christian doctrine advise? According to Sartre, it directs us to 'Act with charity, love your neighbour, deny yourself for others, choose the way which is hardest, and so forth' (EH, p. 355). Will this advice be helpful? Sartre doubts it. Rather than settling the question, he argues, this advice simply opens up new questions and leaves us without guidance as to how to answer them. To whom should this young man direct his neighbourly love: his mother or his compatriots? To whom is more charity owed? For which others ought he to deny himself? Which is the harder road? There is no way, Sartre argues, to answer these questions in advance. The Christian doctrine therefore leaves us exactly as badly off as we were before, in exactly the situation that the existentialist held us always to be: having to choose, without reason, justification or excuse for our choice.

Sartre does not address the consequentialist argument explicitly, but a comment of his suggests the stance he would take towards such a view. The consequentialist argues that we ought to act in such a way as to bring about the best consequences, as measured by the amount of happiness that results, or the balance of satisfied preferences over unsatisfied. Very well, but how are we to calculate these consequences? The young man faces the choice of almost certainly satisfying his mother's preferences by staying, or taking the chance that he might contribute to the happiness and preference satisfaction of a great many French people by going. How do we weigh the almost certain satisfaction of one preference against the contribution that going to join the FFF might make to the satisfaction of many? There are two variables to consider in making the calculation: the probability of achieving the ends set, and the weight of the various preferences. Both seem simply impossible to measure. Thus, Sartre concludes, no one can give an answer *a priori* to the question:

> Which is the more useful aim, the general one of fighting in and for the whole community, or the precise aim of helping one particular person to live? (EH, p. 355)

It ought to be pointed out here that though Sartre's criticism is relevant and valid, in that consequentialists do indeed owe us an account of how to calculate probability and – harder still – how to weigh preferences against each other, this ought not to be Sartre's most fundamental criticism of consequentialism. Prior to these essentially practical questions, there is a more fundamental issue: why should we care more about preference satisfaction (or happiness, or welfare, or whatever else the consequentialist chooses as the good to be maximized) than anything else? Consequentialists think that it is obvious that we ought to care so, but it really isn't so obvious at all. One doesn't need to bring to bear all the value scepticism of an existentialist to see this. It might genuinely satisfy the preferences of an alcoholic to pour her another drink; but it is, at the very least, not obvious that pouring her another drink will be the best action to perform. A world in which everyone was permanently tranquillized by narcotics might very well be much happier than this world; nevertheless, it is not clearly a better world. A world ruled by a benevolent dictator might conceivably be administered so that people's welfare is looked after better than in a world in which we are all responsible for deciding the course of our own lives and the shape of our society; for all that, it is far from obvious that the former would be a more desirable world.

Sartre's opposition to consequentialism will ultimately rest on an even more radical objection. It is simply false that there are any values that are normative for me independent of my free choice. If I claim that there are such values, I am attempting to evade responsibility for my choices. I can, if I wish, choose to be a consequentialist and make all my most important decisions in the light of their probable consequences. I can take the welfare or happiness of others as my supreme value. But if I am to do so authentically, I must recognize that there is no sense in which I *had* to do so, that my ethical stance depends on nothing more solid, nothing more certain than my free choice.

Having dispensed with consequentialism, Sartre then turns to its traditional adversary, deontology. What would a Kantian have us do, he asks? As we have seen, Kant believed we ought to be guided by the categorical imperative, and it is therefore to this that Sartre turns. He refers, however, to a different formulation of the imperative than that which we examined above. This formulation states,

> Act in such a way that you always treat humanity, whether in your own person or in the person of any other, never simply as a means, but always at the same time as an end.

This version of the categorical imperative forbids us to use other people simply as a means to our ends. It is, of course, permissible to use them as means, so long as at the same time you treat them as ends. It is permissible for me to use the work of the farmer as a means to my satisfying my need for food, so long as I also recognize that farmer as an end herself – perhaps by paying her for her labour, thereby allowing her to achieve her ends.

Kant claims that this version of the categorical imperative is equivalent to the one we examined earlier (which stated that an action was morally permissible so long as it was universalizable). Perhaps the thought is that this second version is derivable from the first: since I wish to be always treated as an end, I am committed, by the universalizability principle, to treating others as ends as well. In any case, the principle is clearly deontological: it sets limits to the kinds of actions I can perform by reference to my duties, and not the consequences of my actions.

Will the categorical imperative offer Sartre's pupil any guidance? Sartre doubts it. It tells him to treat others as ends, and never only as means. But in this case, both courses of action available to him will treat someone as a means and someone else as an end. If the young man stays with his mother, he certainly treats her as an end. At the same time, however, he treats the soldiers of the Free French Forces as a means only; a means to the goal he shares of the liberation of France. At the same, however, 'the converse is also true':

> if I go to the aid of the combatants I shall be treating them as the end at the risk of treating my mother as a means. (EH, p. 355)

Thus the categorical imperative does not single out a *unique* action as the one that ought to be performed. But if it does not single out a unique action, it leaves Sartre's pupil without any guidance at all.

Would the first version of the categorical imperative fare any better? Sartre does not address the question, but let's pause to consider it ourselves. This version states, you will remember, that we must only perform acts that are based on a maxim that we could rationally universalize. Now, which course of action meets this test? Ought we to will that young men should always aid their aged mothers? Or ought we to will that young men should, if able to do so, always fight to liberate their country from oppressive invaders? It seems that we will want to universalize *both* propositions – which leaves us precisely as badly off as we were before.

Sartre considers one final strategy to lift the burden of choice. The young man tried to put his trust in his instincts. He would see what his feelings directed him to do, and resolve his dilemma in this manner. If philosophical theories cannot make his decision for him, then perhaps internal impulses, drives and sentiments will take their place. Thus the young man resolves to act on his stronger feeling. Will his love for his country or for his mother prevail?

Will this strategy succeed where the others failed, and relieve Sartre's pupil of the need to make an unjustifiable choice? Once again, Sartre denies that it will. As we have seen, nothing can inhabit consciousness – not even an emotion. If I feel an emotion, it is because I sustain that emotion in being by making it the object of intentional consciousness. In the end, to say that I feel an emotion is to say that I choose to feel it.

Sartre develops this point by asking, 'how does one estimate the strength of a feeling?' (EH, p. 355) I can know how strong my feeling is only by its motivating power. Thus, I will know whether my love for my country or my love for my mother is the stronger by seeing which I will be motivated to act upon. If I stay with my mother, I will know that my love for her is the stronger. But if it is only my action which reveals to me the strength of my feeling, I cannot appeal to the strength of that feeling in order to guide my action. Once again, it is left up to me to choose: to choose how to act, and at the same time to choose which feeling will be the stronger.

Thus, Sartre concludes, I cannot find a guide that will relieve me of my burden of choice, neither within me nor without. How, then, ought we to regard the actions of Sartre's pupil in coming to ask him for advice? Surely this course of action is always open to each of us, and surely by asking for advice we lift the burden of radical responsibility from our shoulders?

Once again, Sartre denies that this strategy for evading responsibility can succeed. In fact, Sartre's pupil has already made a choice: he has chosen his adviser, and thereby the advice that he will receive. He could have chosen a priest instead of Sartre; if he had, he might have chosen either a collaborationist priest or one who sympathized with the Resistance. In either case, he would have chosen the kind of advice he would get. And if, to circumvent this problem, the young man had chosen his adviser at random, he would still be faced with the necessity of choosing whether to accept this advice or not.

Can I opt out of choice altogether? Can I relieve myself of my burden of radical freedom by simply refusing *all* the alternatives that offer themselves? Can our young man decide not to choose between his mother and his country? Sartre denies that not choosing is a possibility, and he seems to be on strong ground here. What would it mean for me not to choose? Would it not, in fact, constitute yet another choice – one as unjustifiable as any other, and, moreover, one as value laden as any other? Consider Sartre's pupil once more: either he stays with his mother, or he leaves. There is no third possibility. Similarly, either he joins the Free French Forces or he doesn't. He might leave his mother *without* joining the FFF; perhaps the options he has sketched are not the only ones available to him. Nevertheless, to act so will still constitute acting upon a decision. He will, necessarily, have chosen.

Whatever he decides, his choice will entail the choice of values. The refusal to act, if it were possible, implies that the world is not so objectionable that it ought to be changed: it implies that the effort it would take to change the world is not worth the potential gains. In choosing not to act, I have chosen just as absolutely as if I had taken any other course of action.

We cannot, therefore, divest ourselves of the radical burden of choice. It is always up to us to choose, and to choose the values that will justify our choice. We make our choice without guidance, without justification or excuse. Sartre's advice to his pupil reflected this fact: 'I had but one reply to make. You are free, therefore choose – that is to say, invent' (EH, p. 356).

FURTHER READING

Kant's most accessible exposition of his moral theory is his *Groundwork of the Metaphysics of Morals*, trans. Mary Gregor (Cambridge: Cambridge University Press, 1998). Aristotle's virtue ethics is developed in the *Nichomachean Ethics* and elsewhere. Confucian virtue ethics stems from the *Analects*, trans. Simon Leys (New York: W.W. Norton, 1997). Kant's reply to Benjamin Constant is 'On a Supposed Right to Lie from Altruistic Motives', in *Ethics*, ed. Peter Singer (Oxford: Oxford University Press, 1994).

Bernard Williams and J.C.C. Smart's *Utilitarianism: For and Against* (Cambridge: Cambridge University Press, 1973) is a classic example of the polemics concerning the potentially counter-intuitive implications of consequentialism. The example of the sheriff's dilemma is taken from H.J. McCloskey, 'An Examination of Restricted Utilitarianism', *Philosophical Review*, 66, 1957, pp. 466–85; reprinted in many anthologies.

For a recent introduction to all three major ethical systems – consequentialism, deontology, and virtue ethics – see Marcia Baron, Philip Pettit and Michael Slote, *Three Methods of Ethics: A Debate* (Oxford: Blackwell, 1997).

Authenticity and bad faith

Sartre holds that nothing can ever divest us of the burden of radical responsibility for our choices. Nevertheless, most of us most of the time will attempt to refuse this burden. We will attempt to find excuses, reasons, causes – forces that determine us from within or without to act in a certain manner, or justifications that select our action as the only one rationally or morally open to us. To the extent that we think that we have succeeded in finding such excuses or justifications, Sartre argues, we are in bad faith.

To understand bad faith, perhaps it would be helpful to return to the example of the homosexual I sketched earlier. As I noted at the time, I altered that example slightly in order to bring out the implications of Sartre's anti-essentialism. In my version, the point of the example was to demonstrate how the for-itself is always beyond any essence; how nothing, not even its sexuality, could ever constitute a nature for it. In Sartre's own use of the example, however, the homosexual is in bad faith, precisely *because* he makes exactly this claim. That is, the homosexual is a victim of a kind of self-deception, in so far as he asserts that he is *not* a homosexual.

But surely Sartre has provided the homosexual with the philosophical warrant to deny that he is a homosexual. How can Sartre accuse him of self-deception for simply asserting the conclusion that Sartre himself has devoted so many pages to establishing? When we examine exactly what the homosexual asserts, the question becomes all the more pressing. For Sartre's homosexual, though recognizing all 'his faults',[16] nevertheless

> struggles with all his strength against the crushing view that his mistakes constitute for him a *destiny*. He does not wish to let himself be considered as a thing. He has an obscure but strong feeling that an homosexual is not an homosexual as this table is a table or as this red-haired man is red-haired ... Does he not recognize in himself the peculiar, irreducible character of human reality? (BN, p. 64)

The answer to this last question is, of course, yes. The homosexual is quite right in holding that he is not a homosexual in the same sense as a table is a table. A table, as we have seen, is an object; that is, it is the kind of thing that has an essence. But a person does not have an essence. It is not in his nature to *be* homosexual (or heterosexual), because he does not have a nature at all.

But if this is the case, then how is the homosexual the victim of bad faith? Sartre contends that though the homosexual's view includes a 'comprehension of truth' (BN, p. 64), nevertheless the claim that we are not what we are is open to abuse. It is abused when it is used to deny that the acts we have committed in the past, the character traits we have exhibited and the decisions we have taken make us the kinds of people we are. Earlier, we distinguished between a shallow and a deep sense of being. We said that in the deep sense – the sense in which tables are table, or in which cats have it in their nature to hunt – the for-itself is not anything at all. But in the shallower sense of being, the sense that makes it true that I am an Australian, or that someone else is a company executive, being is usefully and truthfully ascribed to us. What the homosexual is doing, in insisting that he is not gay, is playing on the word 'being'. His claim that he is not homosexual is true if it is taken as meaning that homosexuality is not in his nature. It is true, that is, if the word 'being' is taken in its deep sense. But the homosexual here uses the assertion that he is not gay to claim something quite different; that he is not gay in the shallow sense of 'being'. This is simply untrue; it denies, falsely, that a pattern of behaviour can be ascribed to him.

To put the point in another way, we must take every occurrence of the word 'is' in Sartre's formula seriously. The for-itself really *is* what it *is not* and *is not* what it nevertheless *is*. The homosexual claims – truthfully – that he *is not* what he is (that is, gay), in a deliberate (though not entirely conscious) attempt to deny that nevertheless he *is* what he is not.

It is characteristic of bad faith to play off one aspect of ourselves against another. The person in bad faith will typically identify herself wholeheartedly with one of her characteristics – with her (shallow) being to the exclusion of her (deep) nonbeing, or vice versa. Sartre calls these two aspects of the self 'facticity' and 'transcendence'. 'Facticity' refers to all those elements of ourselves to which it is possible truthfully to ascribe being: our past actions, our character, our bodily existence and our situation in the world (French, English, middle class, female and so on). In other words, our facticity refers to those aspects of ourselves which are factual. Our 'transcendence', on the other hand, is that aspect of ourselves which permits us always to be beyond our facticity. It refers to the fact that a nothingness always intervenes between our facticity and ourselves, in such a manner that we can never be reduced to mere facticity. It refers, that is, to our essential freedom. Someone is in bad faith to the extent that they affirm their facticity at the expense of their transcendence or vice versa. Thus, bad faith is

> a certain art of forming contradictory concepts which unite in themselves both an idea and the negation of that idea. The basic concept which is thus engendered utilizes the double property of the human being, who is at once a *facticity* and a *transcendence*. These two aspects of human reality are and ought to be capable of a valid coordination. But bad faith does not wish either to coordinate them or to surmount them in a synthesis. (BN, p. 56)

Rather than synthesize or coordinate these two irreducible aspects of ourselves, bad faith attempts to affirm one at the expense of the other.

Thus bad faith has two faces: it either affirms our transcendence at the expense of our facticity, or affirms our facticity at the expense of our transcendence.[17] So far, we have examined only one of these faces. The homosexual affirmed his transcendence, in order to deny his facticity. We ought, however, to expect to find the other kind of bad faith more common, the kind that affirms facticity at the expense of transcendence. After all, it was only as the outcome of a lengthy and demanding philosophical investigation that Sartre was in a position to affirm that the existence of the for-itself precedes its essence. In fact, it is somewhat surprising to find that bad faith *ever* comes in this 'existentialist' form. How is it that someone, like the homosexual in Sartre's example, is able to affirm transcendence in this way, if not as a result of having read Sartre?

The solution to this puzzle lies in what Sartre calls our 'pre-ontological comprehension' of our being. Though it is true that demanding philosophical work is needed before we can show how and why it must be true that the for-itself is irreducibly both transcendence and facticity, that it is the being that is what it is not and is not what it is, nevertheless each of us already senses this fact about ourselves. It is not simply a philosophical mistake to say that human beings have a nature or an essence, or to say that all our actions are determined. In addition to being a philosophical mistake, it is an act of bad faith. It is a paradigm case of the kind of bad faith that is the polar opposite of that in which the homosexual was engaged; the kind of bad faith that affirms our facticity at the expense of our transcendence. We will find, Sartre would say, that when a philosopher advances such a position, she is in bad faith, which is to say that we will find a motivation for her position in her psychic life. It is in order to deny an aspect of herself that a philosopher will deny human transcendence.

What kind of motive might someone have to deny their own transcendence? Sartre holds that we each have a very strong motivation to do so. To be transcendent is, Sartre argues, to be free, in a very radical sense. To be free in this sense is to be so constituted that everything is up to us. We are free not only to make choices, but more radically to decide the meaning of our choices. But to be so free is a crushing burden. It implies that nothing beyond my choice justifies that choice; there is nothing to which I can appeal beyond my freedom in order to show that my choice is the right one. Moreover, to be free in this radical sense is a burden that can never be lifted. I am not free now and again, or with regard to this or that. I am free all the time and in every one of my acts. I am never forced to do *anything*. To think I am is to be in bad faith.

Since we have a pre-ontological comprehension of our transcendence, we sense our freedom, in all its depth. We know that our actions are up to us to decide, without justification or excuse. Our freedom is revealed to us by way of an emotion: anguish.

Why is the revelation of my freedom accompanied by an almost overwhelming feeling of anguish? Yet another of Sartre's vivid examples will throw light on the phenomenon (BN, p. 30). Sartre asks us to interrogate the experience of vertigo. Here I am on a narrow path, a path without a guardrail, which skirts the edge of a precipice. My first emotional response to my precarious situation will probably be fear: fear that I might slip and fall to my death. I respond to my fear with greater care. I examine the surface of the path and look out for loose stones that might cause me to lose my footing; I keep as far as possible from the edge of the path, and so on.

Thus far, I experience no anguish. I experience my situation in anguish when I reflect upon the measures I have taken to avoid falling and realize with horror that my situation – inching along a dangerous path – is not sufficient to motivate my prudence. The path, with its precipitous drop, did not after all necessitate my conduct. It did not *cause* me to take extra care. To see this, we might represent my behaviour as the outcome of a piece of practical reasoning – perhaps even an Aristotelian practical syllogism:

Premise 1. If I fall from this path, I will certainly die.
Premise 2. Preserving my life is of the first importance to me.
Conclusion: I ought to take every precaution against falling.

This is a perfectly sound piece of reasoning, one that moreover may well represent, in explicit and propositional form, precisely the kind of reasoning in which we all habitually engage. Given the premises, the conclusion follows with all the necessitating force of logic. *But*, Sartre will ask, what necessitates the premises? In particular, does anything make it *necessarily* the case that my life is of the first importance to me? Some philosophers have held that the answer is yes. Those who are convinced by sociobiological arguments, for example, might think that it is simply a fact about human beings that they are strongly motivated to preserve their lives, to the exclusion of anything else. But this is a difficult position to sustain, in the face of widespread evidence that human beings will sacrifice their lives for any number of reasons. Given that this is the case (and of course given the Sartrean argument that there are no such facts about human beings, nothing that causes them to act as they do), Sartre concludes that it is in fact our free choice which confers on premise 2 whatever force it has. Thus the whole piece of reasoning is predicated on human freedom; nothing necessitates our taking extra care to preserve our lives.

Sartre thinks that when we grasp this simple fact, we are gripped by anguish. I suddenly realize that I do not *have* to preserve my life; I have as much reason to throw myself over the precipice as I do to take extra care to avoid slipping. All reasons, all the weight on either side of the question, depend upon my freedom, and nothing else: 'If *nothing* compels me to save my life, *nothing* prevents me from precipitating myself into the abyss' (BN, p. 32). My anguish – here revealed through my feeling of vertigo – arises as I suddenly realize that it is up to me to decide, without justification or excuse.

The experience of vertigo is paradigmatic of anguish because anguish, like vertigo, is the feeling that arises when I am without 'guardrails'. All at once I grasp the fact that there are no barriers in consciousness. My behaviour is never determined, neither by external causes nor by internal obstacles. Whenever I act, the meaning of my actions must always be traced back to my free choice.[18]

It is this feeling of anguish, this feeling that haunts us whenever we realize how absolute is our freedom, which provides us with our motivation to deny our transcendence. It is reassuring, somehow, to think that we *must* act as we do; that I have no choice but (to get up when the alarm clock rings, to take extra care when traversing a dangerous path, simply to go on living). It provides us with the ultimate in excuses, an excuse somewhat akin to that relied upon by so many Nazi officers: 'I was only following orders.' If we could establish that our actions were necessitated (by our biology, our environment, our history), the burden of radical freedom would be lifted.

But in fact nothing will lift this burden, and we are in bad faith to the extent that we try to cast off our freedom.

Thus far, we have given only one of the two conditions that must be met before we are justified in saying that someone is in bad faith. We have seen that in order for someone to be in bad faith, they must be engaging in the enterprise of attempting to deny some irreducible aspect of their being in order to identify themselves wholly with another aspect. But this description is compatible with barefaced lying. Being in bad faith is not lying, or at least it is not *simply* lying. I am in bad faith when I am the victim of self-deception; when I lie to *myself*.

There is an immediate conceptual problem: how is it possible to lie to oneself? Sartre's own analysis of the lie demonstrates the difficulty. Lying requires that the liar knows the truth and intends to deceive his listener. If he does not know the truth, he is not lying. If the information that I impart to you turns out to be utterly false, but I do not know that when I tell it to you, I am not lying. Perhaps I am entirely sincere in believing what I say, in which case my ignorance might be condemned, but not my veracity. Perhaps I ought not to pretend I know what I claim to know, because I have insufficient information upon which to base my suppositions, but in that case we must say that I show a reckless disregard for the truth, not that I am (straightforwardly) a liar.

Thus the liar must know the truth.[19] In addition, he must know that he lies. He must believe that his words will be interpreted by his listener in such a manner as to mislead. If I *intend* to convey the truth to you, but my words are misinterpreted by you in such a manner that you come to believe something that is false, we will not say that I have lied. Once again, there might be grounds for holding me culpable – of carelessness, perhaps. But I am not guilty of lying.

In order to lie, then, the liar must be in possession of the truth (or at least believe himself to be), and intend to mislead his listener regarding that truth. These are the conditions that must be met on the part of the liar. Let's now turn to the matching conditions upon the part of his listener. In order to be lied successfully to, so to speak, I must meet the following conditions: I must not know the truth and I must believe my interlocutor to be in possession of it.

Moreover, I must believe that he is sincere in what he says. If none of these conditions is met, I will not be convinced by the lie. I will not be successfully lied to.

Given all these conditions of lying, it is easy to see how one person might lie to another. There is no conceptual difficulty in understanding how one person might know the truth and yet act so as deliberately to mislead another. Nor is there any difficulty in understanding how someone who is ignorant of the truth might be misled by a convincing performance. But how is it possible to lie to *oneself*? How, that is, is it possible for someone to know the truth but refrain from disclosing it to themselves? In order to lie, I must know the truth and know that I am lying. In order to be successfully lied to, however, I must *not* know the truth and must believe the liar to be sincere. How are these contradictory conditions to be met within the unity of a single consciousness?

The most obvious solution to this problem is to suppose an internal division within consciousness, a division that will enable one part of consciousness to play the role of the liar while another part plays that of the lied-to. If we adopt this solution, then the problem simply dissolves: one part of consciousness could know and intend to deceive, while the other could fail to know and be deceived. The Freudian architectonic of consciousness, with its division of the self into three relatively independent parts, could therefore explain self-deception with little trouble.

But the Freudian approach, or indeed any that admits divisions within consciousness, is not open to Sartre. As we have seen, Sartre denies that anything can ever be within consciousness – there are no drives, no barriers and certainly no divisions within it. Instead, consciousness is 'translucent'; entirely open to its own view.

Sartre will therefore face special difficulties in accounting for the possibility of bad faith. On the other hand, it might be that his account is capable of being more sensitive to the contradictory demands of the concept of self-deception than is the Freudian. The Freudian account is hardly an account of *self*-deception at all (or, if it is, then it faces the same problems as the Sartrean analysis). If the Freudian supposes that consciousness is really divided into separate parts, then she can account for the *deception* in self-deception easily and naturally. But to the extent that the fact of division is meant to be taken seriously, she risks losing the *self* from the picture. If the deceiver is really distinct from the deceived, we are confronted with a simple case of lying – a peculiar case, admittedly, in that the liar and the lied-to inhabit one and the same body, but we would nevertheless hesitate before we said that they were one and the same *person*. There must be a distinction between genuine self-deception – which is, after all, an everyday phenomenon – and the experience of people who suffer from multiple personality disorder (if indeed there are any). Someone whose body is, at it were, inhabited by several different people could meet the Freudian conditions for self-deception. One of his 'personalities' might know something and set out to deceive another of his personalities; he might even succeed in this enterprise (perhaps he leaves notes for that other personality). Nevertheless, the fact that these personalities inhabit one and the same body does not suffice to show that we are dealing with a genuine case of *self*-deception.

If there is to be self-deception, then, the divisions within the self must not be too sharp. Perhaps the Freudian might attempt to rescue the sense in which the deceiver and the deceived are the same person, by insisting that the barriers between the parts of the self are not in fact insuperable. But to the extent she does so – that is, to the extent to which she is justified in attributing self-deception to a single self – the paradox of self-deception returns. We are once more faced with the problem of how it can be that one and the same consciousness can play the roles of the deceiver and the deceived simultaneously. Thus, Sartre might say, either the Freudian cannot account for self-deception at all, or, to the extent that she is able to, it will be by reference to Sartrean, and not Freudian, notions. In particular, Sartre says, it must be the case that the agency – Sartre calls it the 'censor' – in the Freudian unconscious which is responsible for repression and for resisting the attempts of the analyst to bring the cause of neuroses to light must both know what it is that is to be repressed and deny that it knows this. Which is to say that 'the censor is in bad faith' (BN, p. 53).

Thus far, we have not shown how self-deception is possible on the Sartrean view. We have, however, given some reasons why this view might not face any difficulties peculiar to it; self-deception (if indeed it exists) just is a paradoxical concept. No account of it will be sufficient which cannot explain how one and the same *self* can simultaneously be the deceiver and the deceived.

Let's turn, now, to the details of Sartre's solution to the problem of self-deception. We have already glimpsed the outlines of part of the solution. We saw that bad faith plays off aspects of our being against other aspects; our transcendence against our facticity. The first thing to notice about self-deception that proceeds in this manner is that it does not attempt to assert anything that is simply false. The homosexual, in Sartre's example, does not lie. He acknowledges his past relationships. He simply insists that nevertheless he is not a homosexual because, as a for-itself, he can never be anything at all. Similarly, a person who attempts to affirm her facticity at the expense of her transcendence will not – simply – engage in a falsehood. In insisting upon certain aspects of herself – her biology, her history, her dispositions and character – she may really be pointing to facts about herself. Someone who is in bad faith is able to be convinced by the evidence presented precisely because it is partially true.

A person in bad faith does not ask herself to believe a falsehood, then; she simply takes a part of the truth for the whole. Bad faith is not just self-deception; it is also *faith*. Someone is in bad faith when they decide to accept a low standard of evidence for a proposition; when they engage themselves to be convinced by scanty proof. This shows, Sartre says, that the project of bad faith must *itself* be in bad faith. Before I have the evidence for the proposition I wish to believe, I must have *already* decided to be convinced by that evidence (and, conversely, to ignore the evidence that weighs against it). I am able to be in bad faith – rather than simply pretending to believe something I know full well not to be true – at this antecedent level because once again the project of bad faith does not require me to believe a falsehood. I can consent to being convinced by little evidence, secure in the knowledge that with regard to the kinds of questions about which it is possible to be in bad faith – questions about myself and my character, my past and my future – we are always in the realm of probability. There are no absolutely undeniable proofs here, I can tell myself, and thus be reassured that my decision to be convinced by *this* evidence, while ignoring all of *that*, is in fact in good faith.

Bad faith thus plays off truth against truth it affirms one true proposition at the expense of another. We cannot engage in bare-faced acts of self-deception with regard to ourselves, but we can convince ourselves to believe half-truths. I can take refuge in the complex and paradoxical structure that constitutes my subjectivity – my being what I am not while yet not being what I am – in order to affirm that I do not believe what I believe. Nevertheless, the fact remains that at some level, I must *know* what it is that I deny, and know that I intend to deceive myself about it. We see here the decisive difference between a Freudian account of self-deception and the Sartrean account. On the Freudian view, I cannot be *blamed* for my repression, nor held responsible for failing to know the content of what is repressed. On the Sartrean view, however, I am responsible all the way down. I know what it is that I do not know, and I know that I am in bad faith in pretending not to know it.

If this is the case, then what will authenticity consist of in the case at hand? Given that I am in bad faith if I identify myself with *either* my transcendence *or* my facticity, how ought I to think of myself at all? Is there an authentic manner of coordinating these irreducible aspects of myself?

Sartre holds that there is. The homosexual must neither simply deny that he is a homosexual (for that would be to deny his facticity) nor simply identify himself with it (which would be denying his transcendence). But there is no reason why he cannot acknowledge both aspects of his being without attempting to reduce himself to either one or the other. That is, the homosexual can, in good faith, assert of himself that

[t]o the extent that a pattern of conduct is defined as the conduct of pederast and to the extent that I have adopted this conduct, I am a pederast. But to the extent that human reality can not be finally defined by patterns of conduct, I am not one. (BN, p. 64)

In so far as he does not attempt to reduce himself to either his transcendence or his facticity, in so far as he does not look for excuses for his behaviour, or reasons that single it out as uniquely rational or moral, in so far as he acknowledges that it is always up to him to decide how to live, what values to uphold, even what meaning to confer on his past, the homosexual can be authentic; he can exhibit the one character trait that is incumbent on us all.

FURTHER READING

In part in response to Sartre's work, there is now a considerable literature on self-deception. A useful collection is Brian P. McLaughlin and Amélie Oksenberg Rorty (eds), *Perspectives on Self-Deception* (Berkeley: University of California Press, 1988). There is also a large literature on the Sartrean solution to the problem, including Ronald Santoni's book-length study, *Bad Faith, Good Faith, and Authenticity in Sartre's Early Philosophy* (Philadelphia: Temple University Press, 1995). Phyllis Sutton Morris, 'Self-Deception: Sartre's Resolution of the Paradox', in *Jean-Paul Sartre: Contemporary Approaches to His Philosophy*, ed. Hugh J. Silverman and Frederick A. Elliston (Pittsburgh: Duquesne University Press, 1980), and Robert V. Stone, 'Sartre on Bad Faith and Authenticity', in *The Philosophy of Jean-Paul Sartre*, ed. Paul Arthur Schilpp (La Salle, ILL: Open Court, 1981) deserve special mention.

For a short but penetrating discussion of the attractions of the notion of authenticity in general, see Charles Taylor, *The Ethics of Authenticity* (Cambridge, MA: Harvard University Press, 1992).

Freedom

We now have a bare-bones sketch of Sartre's thought before us. It is time to deepen the picture. We will follow Sartre as he shows how the for-itself chooses its world and itself. We will see him claim, moreover, that his theory of radical freedom gives us the means to understand the individual person.

Let me start, once again, with one of Sartre's own illuminating examples. Sartre asks us to imagine the following situation:

> I start out on a hike with friends. At the end of several hours of walking my fatigue increases and finally becomes very painful. At first I resist and then suddenly I let myself go, I give up, I throw my knapsack down on the side of the road and let myself fall down beside it. (BN, p. 453)

What has happened in this completely everyday scenario? How are we to think of this – has our hiker been *overcome* with fatigue, so that he acted as he had to, or has he freely *chosen* to rest?

How are we to decide this question? Sartre notes that the other hikers have not given into their fatigue; they keep walking until they reach their previously selected campsite. But they are no fitter than I am; they are about the same age and are about as active as I am. Thus, it is reasonable to conclude that they are as tired as I am. How, then, does it happen that I find my fatigue intolerable, so that I say it *made* me stop, and they are able to continue walking? Am I right when I claim that my tiredness *caused* me to stop walking?

As we have seen, Sartre denies that causality operates upon human behaviour. Though it is certainly the case that physical causes operate upon my *body* – lack of food will eventually cause my death, for example – nothing causes me to *act* in this way or that. So it seems that my claim must be false: my tiredness did not cause my stopping.

Surely, however, this cannot be the whole story. Even if we want to agree with Sartre here, and conclude that my tiredness did not cause me to stop, nevertheless we can easily imagine situations in which our actions *are* caused. Sometimes, we think, our emotions just take over and we act without thinking. Think of someone who wakes to find her room engulfed in flames. She will simply flee in terror. Her actions, we will want to say, were caused by her fear, and her fear, in turn, by the fire.

We might think, perhaps, that some of our actions are free, whereas others are determined. Sometimes we are given the mental space in which to decide rationally what to do; at other times we are forced to act without thinking, and then we simply do what our emotions dictate. Tempting though this picture is, Sartre holds that it is fundamentally confused. We need to clarify our thinking, Sartre holds, in order to eliminate this confusion. And the way to do this is to examine this concept that we have been applying so unreflectively up till now. What is a cause? What do we mean when we say that an action was caused?

Obviously, we do not think that human actions are caused in the same sense as are purely physical events. Human *movements* can be so caused – we can cause someone's arm to move by passing an electric current through it, for example – but movements so caused do not count as actions. I am not guilty of assault if my arm hits someone when it is so moved, but only if I have acted to hit someone. Nevertheless, we do speak of the causes of genuine actions. For example, historians frequently speak of causes as they operate in history. Think of books with titles like *The Causes of the Second World War*. Wars are historical events that are decomposable, in some sense, into individual human actions. In what sense, however, can these actions be caused?

Let's examine this question by way of a historical example. How does a historian go about explaining a historical event? Let's take as our example Napoleon's defeat in Russia. Generally speaking, historians believe that the most satisfying explanation invokes *objective* factors – that is, features of the world. Thus a historian might point to Napoleon's extended supply lines, which made it difficult to keep his armies provisioned, or the ferocity of the Russian winter, which took a heavy toll on the retreating French soldiers. But she might also need to invoke *subjective* factors; states of mind of the historical actors. Thus she might point to the intense patriotism and unity of the Russian people as an explanatory factor.

Human actions always need to be understood by reference to both sets of features, Sartre believes. Whether we are explaining great historical dramas or the smallest incident in daily life, a full explanation must invoke both. Very often, however, we explain human actions sufficiently well by reference to just one. A banal example will make the point clear. Suppose you and a friend are sitting together watching television. Suddenly your friend gets up and walks to the kitchen. Now, if you asked him for an explanation of his action, you would probably be satisfied by him telling you that there is a drink in the fridge. He is invoking only one of the two factors we said constituted an explanation of human action – in this case, an objective feature of the world. Nevertheless, his explanation is sufficient for the purposes at hand; you do not need anything added to it to understand his action. This is not because this action doesn't require subjective states for it to be comprehensible, but because the subjective state in question – his being thirsty – is so common that we can simply assume it.

Thus, though very often we only invoke one class in giving explanations, actions can be fully explained only by reference to *both* features of the situation *and* desires of the actor. We can call both of these factors the 'causes' of the action, though we need to be clear when we use this word that we do not thereby intend something akin to the causes of physical events.[20]

Thus, Sartre argues, all actions have two causes. From now on, we will adopt his terminology, and distinguish between the external cause of the action – that is, the situation – which, following the translator of *Being and Nothingness*, we will term the 'cause', and the internal cause, which we will call the 'motive'. The cause of your friend's action was the drink in the fridge; his motive was his thirst.

Now, Sartre asks us to notice something important about both these factors which combined result in action. Both depend, he claims, on the ability of the for-itself to 'nihilate' the world. It is perhaps easiest to get at what Sartre means by this technical term by continuing our example. When you asked your friend for an explanation of his behaviour, he told you he was getting a drink. Now, it is important to see that neither his subjective state – his being thirsty – nor the objective situation – there being a drink in the fridge – are sufficient to motivate his action. In order for him to act, he must nihilate his thirst. That is, he must in some way go beyond it, transcend it. It must not be something that he simply suffers, but something he believes he can change. In this way, his thirst becomes negated, first in thought, then in practice.

Thus the ability of the for-itself to engage in even the most banal of actions rests upon its ability to nihilate the given. To nihilate the given is to separate oneself from it, to negate it. The for-itself is able to do this because, as we have seen, the for-itself secretes nothingness. The world can be transcended, because the for-itself is the being by which nothingness comes to the world.

We have seen how this ability functions in a banal case; now let us examine its functioning in a more significant example. Sartre believes that the ability to nihilate not just our subjective states, but also objective states of the world explains the ability of a people to rise up against its rulers. What is more, it also gives us the means to explain the *failure* of a people so to revolt. Historians have often been puzzled by the fact that the less harshly oppressed will frequently be quicker to revolt than the more. It is, Sartre thinks, a difference in ability to nihilate the situation which explains this apparent anomaly. In general, we accept the historical situation into which we are born; it appears *natural* to us:

In so far as man is immersed in the historical situation, he does not even succeed in conceiving of the failures and lacks in a political organisation or determined economy; this is not, as is stupidly said, because he 'is accustomed to it,' but because he apprehends it in its plenitude of being and because he can not even imagine that he can exist in it otherwise. (BN, p. 434)

In order for us to revolt against our historical situation, first we must nihilate it. But for us to nihilate it, it is necessary that we be able to conceive of a different state of affairs – not as an impossible dream, but as a real possibility. As soon as we are able to do this, we can transcend the objective situation, towards a future state of the world. It is only when we do this that there are causes and motives for us. So long as the Russian peasants, for example, live their situation under the Tsar as *natural*, their hunger is something to be endured. But once they are able to conceive of a different state of affairs, it becomes a *motive* for action, just as their lack of grain becomes a *cause*:

It is on the day that we can conceive of a different state of affairs that a new light falls on our troubles and our sufferings and that we *decide* that these are unbearable. (BN, p. 435)

In order that the world and our subjective states become reasons for action, we must establish a distance between them and ourselves.

With this discussion in mind, let us return to our hiker. He insisted that he *had* to rest. He was too tired, the path was too steep, the sun too hot. His tiredness, we might say, was his motive for stopping, the steepness of the path and the weather were the cause of it. But we have seen Sartre insist that states of the world do not cause human actions. We are now in a position to see that this is doubly true. It is true, first of all, that human actions are never caused in the sense in which mechanical reactions are caused. Actions are never caused in the sense in which one billiard ball hitting another causes that second ball to roll. But it is also true in a second sense. Human actions are certainly motivated and explained by states of the world and facts about people, but in order for these to play their role in motivating action, they must first be nihilated. And the source of that nihilation is always the for-itself itself. It is only in so far as that for-itself projects itself towards another possible state of affairs that the whole ensemble comes to be constituted as causes and motives:

> No factual state whatever it may be … is capable by itself of motivating any act whatsoever. For an act is a projection of the for-itself toward what is not, and what is can in no way by itself determine what is not. (BN, p. 435)

Thus we cannot avoid our ultimate and total responsibility by referring our actions to causes and motives. These only have the force for us which we confer upon them.

If this is the case, however, then we must return to our initial case with a new set of questions in mind. We have seen that nothing causes our hiker to rest, in the sense that physical events are caused. We now know that whatever force the causes and the motives of his action had was due, ultimately, to him. If the sun is too hot, for him and not for the other hikers, it is because he has in some way chosen himself as not being able to tolerate it: 'the for-itself must confer on it its value as cause or motive' (BN, p. 437). The question we must now ask, therefore, is how and why does it happen that this force gets conferred on the causes and the motives of an action, and why are they experienced by all of us as operating upon us, independently of our choices? If I am responsible for the fact that this pain is unbearable, why does it seem to me that it is an alien force intruding upon me without my consent?

It cannot be the case that we choose the force of each cause and each motive as it arises for us. If that were the case, then the behaviour of people would not be as predictable as it is. If we go hiking together and I stop to rest long before we reach the campsite, leaving you waiting impatiently, you will rightly be reluctant to go hiking with me a second time. In all probability (allowing for the intervention of other causes, such as illness), if I once have a much lower level of tolerance for fatigue and for heat than you, I will react the same way again. As we know from our experience – of ourselves, as much as of other people – the behaviour of individuals is very often quite predictable. But if my behaviour is predictable, then I must be reacting in much the same way to the same kinds of situations, which is to say that I must be choosing the same causes and motives and conferring upon them more or less the same kinds of force. I seem to have a standing disposition to behave in a similar way in similar circumstances. I do not, therefore, seem to choose how I will react anew in each such circumstance.

Moreover, the fact that I have such a disposition helps explain why I am not aware of choosing to confer the force that causes and motives have for me. If I were to choose the force of causes and motives each time I acted, it would be difficult for me to conceal this fact from myself. It would not seem to me that I *had* to act as I did. But if I can choose my disposition, in some manner, then the question will not normally arise of what force I ought to confer upon these causes and these motives on this occasion. The work will already have been done, and I will experience the force as coming from the situation and not from me.

We can make sense of our experience, then, by postulating an *initial* choice, which confers on all subsequent causes and motives their value and force. If the initial choice is to have this wide range, it must be a *global* choice. That is, my initial choice cannot be to act in such a way in these (very particular) circumstances. Instead, it must be a choice of the kind of world in which I shall live, and the kind of person I shall be within this world. Sartre calls this the choice of my 'original project'.

The original project

In order to understand this idea, we need to go deeper into Sartre's thought and explore the structure of the for-itself. As we have seen, the for-itself is the being by which nothingness comes to the world. We saw, further, that the being by which nothingness comes to the world must be its own nothingness; that 'by which lack appears in the world must itself be a lack' (BN, p. 87). As Shakespeare noted (to a rather different purpose) in *King Lear*, 'Nothing will come from nothing.' The evidence, for Sartre, that the for-itself is a lack lies in the experience of desire. A being that was simply what it was would be complete in itself and would require nothing in order to complete itself. Only a being that is not in-itself could desire, for desire is, fundamentally, an appeal to something else that it is obscurely felt would complete the self. Thus the desire of the for-itself testifies to its lack of being.

The for-itself experiences itself as a failure, Sartre argues. It wants to *be* – to be a diplomat or a waiter, to have its being suffused with its emotions, to suffer really and fully, and not to suffer from not suffering enough – it wants to coincide with itself, but it is always separated from itself by a nothingness. It always transcends everything it would be, and for that very reason it experiences its being 'as failure *in the presence of* the being which it has failed to be' (BN, p. 89). Thus it is perpetually engaged in the task of pursuing whatever would enable it, once and for all, to be.

Now, if the for-itself is capable of desiring only because it is lacking, if it desires something only in order to complete itself, then what the for-itself lacks must be *itself*. What is missing from the for-itself, what it searches for and desires, is the for-itself as a totality, the for-itself completed. But the for-itself can *never* be completed – not so long as it remains for-itself. A for-itself is defined by the fact that it exists at a distance from itself; it is this division within itself which allows it to be *for*-itself. Thus, if the for-itself were to complete itself, it would be in-itself, not for-itself.

In fact, Sartre maintains, the for-itself *does* seek to be in-itself, but it wants to be *itself* as in-itself. It wants to remain wholly for-itself, while yet also being in-itself. It wants to be for-itself – free and capable of choice – while yet being in-itself, so that its choices will be justified, so that they will have being as their foundation. It wants to be free, and yet capable of being, no longer to suffer from the inability to coincide with itself. It wants to be its own foundation:

> Thus the perpetually absent being which haunts the for-itself is itself fixed in the in-itself. It is the impossible synthesis of the for-itself and the in-itself; it would be its own foundation, not as nothingness but as being and would preserve within it the necessary translucency of consciousness along with the coincidence of itself with being-in-itself. (BN, p. 90)

But the characteristics of the in-itself and the for-itself are incompatible. One is necessarily one or the other, never both at the same time. The for-itself is indeed capable of becoming in-itself; it can and will die. Then it may be said of it that it is what it is. But it will become in-itself only by ceasing to be for-itself.

What the for-itself seeks to be, what Sartre will call the 'in-itself-for-itself', is nothing less than God:

> Is not God a being who is what he is – in that he is all positivity and the foundation of the world – and at the same time a being who is not what he is and who is what he is not – in that he is self-consciousness and the necessary foundation of himself? (BN, p. 90)

This is, of course, an impossible ambition. Nevertheless, it is not an optional one. We cannot give up this project without at the same time ceasing to be a for-itself; a for-itself just is the kind of being who transcends itself towards the in-itself-for-itself. We can abandon this project only when we cease to be the kind of being that is defined by its lack; that is, when we become in-itself and not for-itself. We are all, therefore, engaged in a project in which, as the more reflective among us know, we cannot succeed. As Sartre puts it, in a justifiably famous passage,

> man loses himself as man in order that God may be born. But the idea of God is contradictory and we lose ourselves in vain. Man is a useless passion. (BN, p. 615)

What does this have to do with our hiker, though? Recall our problem: I had shown that the causes and motives of his action must have their force conferred on them by the hiker himself. He chooses the value they will have for him. But we had also seen that this choice cannot be made anew on every single occasion upon which the causes and motives are operative. If this were the case, the hiker would not experience them as coming to him from outside. Thus, I said, the choice must be global and long-lasting, a choice that decides, once and for all, what causes and motives would arise for him. We are now in a position to understand this global choice.

We each face, broadly, the same problem – becoming the in-itself-for-itself, or God. But we each solve the problem in our own way. We each choose a different solution to the problem of being. One person might try to become the in-itself-for-itself by making herself a thing; perhaps by becoming wholly in-itself, yet remaining self-consciousness, she could solve the problem. Other people will have different solutions. Moreover, even when two people adopt what is, at this high level of abstraction, the same solution – to become wholly in-itself, for example – they will each attempt to realize it in a different way. We each sketch our own solution to the problem of being. The only thing all our solutions have in common is that they all fail equally badly.

In any case, our solution will be made in the form of an original choice, of ourselves and of our world. It is this choice of ourselves which confers on everything that we encounter its force and its value for us. It constitutes each of our fundamental projects, in terms of which we will henceforth interpret the world.

Thus, in order to understand the experiences of a person, we need to interpret their actions and feelings, progressively peeling away the layers of meaning until we reach their fundamental choice. Thus our hiker and his companion experience their fatigue differently, each in the light of his own fundamental choice. It is not that the one who wishes to press on does not feel tired. On the contrary, it is, in part, in order to continue experiencing his fatigue that he wants to keep walking. For him, this feeling of tiredness is the instrument by means of which he discovers the world that surrounds him, just as his sunburn is a means of establishing contact with the sun. His suffering is for him a means of *appropriating* the world.

This is not, yet, his fundamental project. We must still interpret the project of appropriation itself, in order that we can reach this most basic of levels. This project of appropriating the world is, Sartre argues, part of the larger project called abandoning oneself to the world, of 'trustingly reassuming it and loving it'. Now, we might abandon ourselves to the world only in order to recover it. By abandoning ourselves to the world, we assert the continuity between ourselves and it, that is, we make ourselves in-itself. We lose our body in fatigue, in order that the in-itself will exist. But we also make ourselves the foundation of the in-itself. Thus we attempt to bring into being a type of in-itself that will also be for-itself. This might be our attempt to solve the problem of being.

What do we accomplish when we interpret someone's behaviour, such as that of our hiker's companion? We have attempted to understand the meaning of his conduct, its place within a larger project. We continue to delve, interpreting each project as a 'secondary structure' within a larger project, until we reach rock bottom, which is 'the original relation which the for-itself chooses with its facticity and with the world':

> But this original relation is nothing other than the for-itself's being-in-the-world inasmuch as this being is a choice. (BN, p. 457)

That is, the original relation of the for-itself to the world stems from its choice of a fundamental project, its solution to the problem of being.

And our hiker himself? What is his fundamental project, and how does it lead him to experience his fatigue as unbearable? Sartre spends less time interpreting his behaviour than that of his companion, but he does say enough for us to begin the interpretive analysis of the hiker's fundamental project. The hiker, Sartre says, distrusts his body. His attitude to it is 'a way of wishing not "to have anything to do with it"'. He wishes to be rid of his fatigue, simply because it incarnates his body, brutally reminding him of his contingency. This rejection of contingency must be interpreted in its turn, until we reach the fundamental project of the for-itself, the hiker's solution to the problem of being. We can speculate that his fundamental choice is of himself as pure for-itself; that he hopes thereby to provide a foundation for his own being and transform himself into the in-itself-for-itself.

We saw earlier how Sartre rejected the Freudian conception of the self as too mechanistic. For Freudian repression he substituted his own notion of bad faith; now he adds to the psychoanalytic tools he has available and sets up existentialism as a rival to Freudianism. For this method of interpreting the experiences and the actions of the for-itself in terms of its fundamental project opens up the possibility of an existential psychoanalysis. Freudian psychoanalysis, Sartre contends, for all its many insights is completely incapable of grasping the individual. Its explanations – in terms of the Oedipus complex and the family romance, of sexuality renounced and repressed – are too global, too broad; they cannot explain why the symptoms of neurosis manifested themselves in just this way for this person, and not for another. It stops too soon, Sartre argues. It might attempt to explain, for example, why Flaubert's ambition manifested itself in literature, and not elsewhere, but the fact of ambition itself it cannot explain. Yet Flaubert's ambition is meaningful and, as such, ought to be explicable. Existential psychoanalysis will go deeper. It will interpret this ambition, and discover its meaning within the complex whole that is Flaubert's life. It will locate the place of this character trait within a larger whole and then interpret that larger whole in turn. It will not stop until it reaches a level beyond which interpretation is no longer possible, a level that is, in a German word that Sartre uses frequently, *selbstständig*; that is, sufficient unto itself.

Every activity, every action, no matter how trivial, is grist to the psychoanalyst's mill. All can be interpreted; any can be a fertile means of gaining access to the fundamental layers of the self. This was Freud's insight, which he put into practice by interpreting slips of the tongue, dreams and habits, and it is an insight that Sartre endorses:

> in each inclination, in each tendency the person expresses himself completely, although from a different angle … But if this is so, we should discover in each tendency, in each attitude of the subject, a meaning which transcends it. (BN, p. 563)

The most trivial of actions can be interpreted, and eventually interpretation will reveal the fundamental project of the for-itself. All our actions are meaningful and the for-itself is a fundamentally comprehensible being.

Sartre does no more than sketch the outlines of the proposed existential psychoanalysis. Its purpose and methodology are left vague. Would this form of psychoanalysis help us to overcome neuroses, or their existential analogues, as Freudian psychoanalysis claims to do? Would it make us happier, as contemporary psychology often claims to do (and, if so, how would the analyst square this ambition with the realization that all our fundamental projects are, on principle, condemned to failure)? Or would it have distinctive goals of its own – perhaps to allow us to live lives that are free of the illusions of bad faith?

It was left to other, later thinkers to attempt the application of Sartrean ideas in a clinical setting. Existential psychoanalysis had a brief heyday in the 1950s and 1960s, though most of its practitioners were more influenced by Heideggerian thought than Sartrean (an influential exception was R.D. Laing, who argued powerfully for the meaningfulness of schizophrenic symptoms). But perhaps its most fruitful application came, not in the clinical setting, but in Sartre's biographies of French writers. In his work on Baudelaire, on Jean Genet and, most brilliantly, on Flaubert, Sartre applied the method he had sketched, frequently to illuminating effect.

In any case, we are now in a position, finally, to describe to what degree and in what manner the for-itself chooses its world. We have seen that this choice cannot be made each time anew; instead, the world is experienced as already meaningful, as already containing causes that interact with my already constituted motives. We can now see to what extent this is indeed true. Once I have made my choice, once I have sketched my solution to the problem of being, everything follows from it. Since I have chosen to experience the in-itself in this manner – as an alien entity, or, on the contrary, as something to be welcomed and assumed – each time it manifests itself I do so experience it. I do not need to reactivate my choice, since I perceive the world through its lens. The world is for me fully meaningful, its causes are demands and my motives entreaties, and the role my free choice has played is hidden from me.

How free is the for-itself?

We never really understand anything in philosophy until we have critically assessed it. Simply describing a position leaves us contemplating it from the outside; it is only when we argue with it that we enter into it and grasp it from within. It is now time, therefore, to grapple with Sartre's theory of radical freedom. How plausible is this picture? And just how free is the for-itself, if this picture is true?

I will take these questions in reverse order, answering the question of the extent of the for-itself's freedom first. Sartre believes that our freedom is total. Nothing limits freedom except freedom itself, he is fond of saying; the only thing I am not free to do is to escape my freedom. But is this notion of absolute freedom coherent? I suspect that it is not. In any case, in the form it takes in Sartre's thought, it does not represent a viable theory.

Let us begin our assessment of Sartre's philosophy of freedom by considering the for-itself as we find it, immersed in its world. This is the situation within which we all find ourselves when we are self-aware enough to reflect on our situation. In this situation, we are not aware of our radical freedom. Instead, as Sartre shows, we experience the world as a space that demands things of us. When my alarm clock rings, its sound for me is an order: I *must* get up. Of course, we now know that this order gets its force from me: its value for me is dependent on a chain of reasons which goes back, ultimately, to my choice of myself and my world. I experience its demand as what Kant called a 'categorical imperative' – an order that I am bound to obey, no matter what I want or believe – but Sartre's analysis has shown that it is in fact a hypothetical imperative; that is, its force depends on a whole series of beliefs and desires of mine, which might have been other than they are.

Thus my alarm clock's demand does not require me to get up, whatever I happen to want. Instead, its command might better be understood as saying, '*If you want to keep your job*, you must get up.' This conditional itself takes its place within a longer chain: 'You must keep your job *if you want to retain the respect of your friends*.' And so on; we can keep tracing the chain of reasons back until we reach the meaning of these activities for me, and, ultimately, the manner in which they take their place within my fundamental project, my solution to the problem of being.

Normally, then, I am not aware of my freedom. I am not aware that these commands, which seem to come to me from the external world, actually have their source in me, and, further, that I can strip them of their force. How, then, does it happen that I become aware of my freedom? How do I come to the realization that I am free to ignore the alarm clock – indeed, free to strip the entire chain of justifications, right down to my fundamental project, of its meaning? How does the worker, who lives his oppression as natural, come to conceive of a different state of affairs, in the light of which he nihilates this one?

The situation itself can *never* be the motive for changing it. 'No factual state whatever it may be … is capable by itself of motivating any act whatsoever' (BN, p. 435). A revolution is not motivated by the poverty of the oppressed masses; such poverty is simply experienced by them as their natural·state. They will not form the project of overthrowing the regime until 'a new light' falls upon their abject state, which shows them the image of a different way of life and holds out the possibility of this way of life for them. Thus, if their poverty falls below the level to which they are accustomed, they easily form the project of reclaiming what they have lost. But if they were born and raised into poverty, the mere continuance of that poverty will not allow them to transcend their situation.

Thus, I can only form the project of changing something – whether it be rearranging my furniture or overthrowing the king – by nihilating the situation, by transcending it towards what it is not. And, as we have seen, nihilation must come from the for-itself. The in-itself is always a plenitude of being; it contains no hollows in which nothingness could lodge. Thus nothingness, the ontological solvent that allows us to establish a distance from being, withdraw from it and transcend it towards something else, must always originate in the for-itself, the being that is its own nothingness.

Thus, we must *first* nihilate the given, and only subsequently does it appear as providing us with causes and motives for changing it. This nihilation is for us a permanent possibility, Sartre insists: at every moment, I have the capacity to strip away the meanings that I have implanted in the world. But we do not, as yet, understand how this might happen. What could possibly motivate me to reject a situation that I experience as natural, if it cannot be that situation itself?

The problem is this: though I might be convinced, abstractly, of Sartre's contention that these meanings have their origin in my choice, and that they are arbitrary, in the sense that they have no more justification than any other set of meanings, nevertheless these *are* the meanings through which I experience the world. They permeate my experiences; everywhere I go I will find them, since they are the lens through which I view my world.

But, if I experience the world through the lens of the meanings I confer upon it, where is there room for me to *choose* between alternatives? Since these alternatives have *already* had their meaning decided – at least implicitly – before they arise for me, I have no choice with regard to them at all. They simply arise for me as causes and motives, and they are causes and motives for me because my fundamental project bestows this force upon them. Consider, then, the situation of our hiker, just before he makes the decision to throw down his knapsack and drop by the side of the road. We may imagine him deliberating as to how he ought to act: 'Should I give in to this tiredness, to this heat? Or should I hold out a little longer?'

We have seen that his tiredness is to be understood, ultimately, in terms of his fundamental project. He apprehends the world through this project, and everything in it is meaningful for him only because the project confers meaning upon it. Thus, he experiences his tiredness as intolerable because his project is such as to lead him to live it in this way. Though it is true that the tiredness owes its significance to him, it receives it only indirectly, by way of its integration into his original project.

As a consequence, the hiker is not free to confer a different meaning upon his tiredness. Or rather, he can do so only by way of a global rejection of his entire original project. Since he does not choose the meaning and value of each entity and experience he has, one by one, but instead chooses a way of being in the world which confers significance upon the things of the world, he can change these significances only by altering this fundamental and original choice.

Sartre insists that our freedom is always absolute. No matter what the situation in which I find myself, I always have a choice. Nothing can force me to act in this way or that. But we can already begin to see that this freedom is in fact heavily qualified. The meanings we discover in the world are conferred upon it by our choices; in this sense, we remain free to alter them by choosing again. But each time we would do so, there is a price to be paid: the renunciation of our entire project. Our hiker cannot choose to resist his fatigue just this once, leaving everything else in place. If the force of his exhaustion indeed comes to him from his project, then resisting it 'just this once' requires the collapse of the project.

Thus we are not free to choose piecemeal. Instead, we choose a project, and experience the world in its terms. I choose a framework in which the world is presented to me, and having made my choice I simply live it. Within the boundaries of a single project, there is no freedom. I cannot choose to alter the significance of any one of my experiences, without at the same time modifying my entire project.

The fact that I cannot choose piecemeal has a surprising consequence. Sartre argues, against the partisans of the thesis that human actions are determined, that our freedom is total. But he seems to deprive himself of what is usually regarded as the strongest argument against the determinist thesis: the fact that we experience our most trivial actions as freely chosen. Indeed, Sartre agrees with the determinists, this everyday experience is a mere illusion. Of course, the form of this thesis will be somewhat different in each case. For those philosophers who deny the existence of free will, human action is the outcome of causal processes that precede it, whether these processes are genetic or environmental (or, more usually, both). As we have seen, Sartre denies that causal processes operate on the for-itself in such a manner as could determine its behaviour. Nevertheless, our everyday experience of free choice is equally illusory for him. If our actions are not the outcome of causal antecedents, nevertheless they are the result of our fundamental project. If physical exhaustion can never determine our hiker to drop by the side of the road, nevertheless the manner in which he has chosen to experience the world is equally effective in compelling his actions.

We can make this clearer by analysing the ordinary experience of making a decision from a Sartrean perspective. Our everyday experience of choice runs something like this:

> I discover myself confronted with two or more alternatives. Each one has something to recommend it, in such a manner that it is not obvious to me which I ought to undertake. I therefore set about a process of deliberation; I weigh the pros and cons of each alternative, and I try to predict the consequences of each. In the best cases, I gradually come to the conclusion that the balance of reasons lies with one of the alternatives, and I therefore opt for it.

The fact that we are prone to experience choice in something like this manner might lead us to see in this experience the paradigmatic locus of free will. For Sartre, on the other hand, to see freedom manifested here, and here alone, is simply bad faith. In fact, there is no freedom in this choice situation.

Notice, first of all, that this choice only arises for me as a result of my project. When we find ourselves confronted with two alternatives between which we must choose, our choice situation itself is circumscribed only against the background of manners of behaving which I take to be given. For example, if I find myself confronted with the choice between two jobs, this is only because I do not (for the moment, at least) question the need for me to have a job at all. In fact, the number of alternatives open to me is much wider than I ever realize. I could choose to take neither job; I could choose to starve, or to commit suicide. Thus, the apparent experience of choice is not the principal locus of human freedom. Instead, it is a severely limited space in which options between which I am relatively indifferent come up for review. Radical choice, if I am indeed capable of such, does not arise in this space. Instead, precisely the opposite happens: the space of decision opens up on the basis of such radical choice.

Thus, the choices that we are aware of ourselves making are relatively trivial, compared with those which we make without conscious deliberation. But we can go still further. We can show not only that these choices are relatively trivial, but that they are not choices at all.

To see this, we need only to recall that the terms in which we make these choices are themselves the product of our fundamental project. When I weigh up the pros and cons of each alternative, this weight, positive or negative, comes to the alternatives from my project. If alternative *A* has in its favour the fact that it pays well, then this has weight for me only in the light of a fundamental project that is such as to confer value on wealth. And so on for all the other characteristics of the alternatives confronting me. Though I experience myself as weighing the alternatives, in fact their weight is not independent of me but comes to them from my choice. Thus it is that a voluntary deliberation is always a deception. How can I evaluate causes and motives on which I myself confer their value before all deliberation and by the very choice which I make of myself? (BN, p. 450)

When I deliberate, I regard myself as assessing the qualities the alternatives possess in themselves. But in so far as these qualities are relevant to my decision, they come to the alternatives from me. Thus, no matter how it may *seem* to me, I do not choose between the alternatives confronting me. Instead, I reveal to myself the consequence of my antecedent fundamental choice.

Thus, within the bounds of a single project, I am not free. Nevertheless, Sartre will insist, I always remain free to choose again. Just as there is no inertia in consciousness, so choices have no momentum of their own. My project owes its existence to me, and persists only to the extent that I reaffirm it. At any moment, I can reject it. Our hiker remains free, Sartre will say. Though his fatigue is not chosen, in the sense that it is merely a consequence of his project, nevertheless the hiker can reject his project and choose again. He can choose to experience the world as a hospitable place, in such a manner that his fatigue is welcome to him as a way of establishing contact with being. Our freedom remains absolute, even though our choices are always total.

Thus, if the for-itself is free, its freedom consists in an ability to choose a fundamental project. It is therefore this ability which we must examine in depth if we are to endorse Sartre's theory of freedom.

We have seen that the meanings of the world are a consequence of our fundamental project. Sartre insists that nevertheless we remain free to reject that project. At any moment I can choose to affirm this project no longer; as I do so, all these meanings will collapse.

But a little reflection on this argument reveals a profound difficulty. Assuming Sartre is right, and that the meaning of my experiences come to me as a consequence of my project, what could possibly motivate me to change this project? When I perceive the world, I am not aware of its significances as coming from myself. To think that I am so aware, or even that I could be in any kind of concrete manner, is to fall back into the objectivist fantasy. The world I experience is a thoroughly human world: I apprehend its significances as simply *there*, independent of my wishes. Thus, even after reading *Being and Nothingness*, I cannot experience my fatigue as chosen. Instead, I live it as manifesting to me what the world is – really – like. My choice is comparable to a pair of tinted spectacles. Though the world takes on the hue it has for me as a result of these lenses, nevertheless it is the world, and not the lens, which I see.

Each of us can perform the experiment for ourselves. Put aside any doubts you might have about Sartre's philosophy, and assume that it is basically correct. Thus the world has the significances it has for you as a result of your fundamental project. All the beauty and all the ugliness you have ever experienced, all the horror and all the wonders you have heard of, all take their value and meaning from you. You are constrained to experience things as you do, given your fundamental project, but you are free to reject that project. Very well; now reject it.

I suspect that you, like me, are left completely at a loss when faced with this demand. When we experience the world through the lens of our project, it is the world which is revealed, and not that project. We do not see, say, the beauty that is revealed to us as originating in us; instead, we see it as objectively there. Now we are faced with the demand to stop seeing this sunset as beautiful; now we are enjoined to experience it as horrific, for instance. Concretely, however, this amounts to the injunction to stop seeing it as it really is and instead see it as something that it is not. We cannot command ourselves to do this, any more than we can command ourselves to believe something we know to be false.

We might usefully compare the interpretation of the world provided to us by our original project with the outlook or world-view shared by members of a culture. We know, abstractly, that many of our perceptions are culturally encoded; we even recognize that some of them are arbitrary, in the sense that we have no good reason to embrace them – rather than those of another culture – other than the simple fact that we were born to them. We know, for example, that what counts as polite behaviour varies from culture to culture, and that what we find offensive might be experienced by members of other cultures as courteous. Though we know this abstractly, the knowledge does little to loosen the grip that our standards of etiquette have upon us. We are not inclined to abandon ours in favour of theirs. If this is the case, however, then how much stronger must be the hold of the interpretation of the world conferred on us by our fundamental project? For we do not experience the latter as arbitrary, nor can we. We have no access to the in-itself except through this significance-conferring perception; it functions for us as the revelation of the properties of the world, not as a screen between us and it. Though we might agree with Sartre, once again abstractly, that this interpretation is due to us, and not to the world, nevertheless we will never have reason to abandon it in favour of another.

We might approach the same point from another direction, by recognizing that every one of my perceptions, every one of my experiences, confirms and reinforces my fundamental project. I can never experience a conflict between it and reality, simply because my perception of reality is always filtered through the project. If I experience my rucksack as too heavy, then this is only because it really is, objectively speaking, too heavy. I have no access to it except via this experience of overwhelming weight. Thus my experience confirms the correctness of the interpretation that flows, ultimately, from my fundamental project. The meanings it imposes upon the world form a closed system, into which nothing can intrude that would disturb it.

For this reason, nothing can happen that would motivate us to change our fundamental project. Nothing can ever provide us with a reason to reject it; on the contrary, every experience, every perception, confirms its validity. As Sartre himself acknowledges,

> our actual choice is such that it furnishes us with no *motive* for making it past by means of a further choice. In fact, it is this original choice which originally causes all causes and all motives which can guide us to partial actions; it is this which arranges the world with its meaning, its instrumental-complexes, and its coefficient of adversity. (BN, p. 465)

Since causes and motives arise only against the background of my choice, since the in-itself cannot motivate any action except in so far as it is understood within the context of a choice, the world can never provide me with reason to reject my fundamental project. Thus, Sartre goes on,

> The absolute change which threatens us from our birth until our death remains perpetually unpredictable and incomprehensible. Even if we envisage other fundamental attitudes as *possible*, we shall never consider them except from outside, as the behaviour of Others. And if we attempt to refer our conduct to them, they shall not for all that lose their character as external and as transcended-transcendences. To 'understand' them in fact would be already to have chosen them. (BN, p. 465)

Sartre expressed the same point a few years earlier, in the diaries he kept while serving in the French army, this time in relation to his own fundamental project. Sartre chose himself as a writer; his own solution to the problem of becoming the in-itself-for-itself was to attempt to objectify himself in the form of books. Thus his life was organized around the project of being a writer. As a consequence, he could not ever seriously contemplate rejecting this project:

> I only ever *dream* of questioning my desire to write, because if I really tried even for an hour to hold it in abeyance, place it in parenthesis, all reason for questioning anything whatsoever would collapse.[21]

Since the fundamental project constitutes a closed and total system, since the entire world is made available for our experience only through its lens, rationally we are unable ever to reject it. Nothing could ever motivate such a rejection. If, then, the project collapses – if, for example, our hiker finds himself able to resist his fatigue, because he now experiences it in terms of a different project – it cannot be as a result of a rational or a conscious decision. Freedom, if there is any in *Being and Nothingness*, hangs from a thread of irrationality. If our project collapses, this can only be the result of a sudden, inexplicable catastrophe that disrupts our world without our cooperation or consent.

But if it is only possible to reject a fundamental project as the result of an inexplicable catastrophe, we are not free to reject our projects at all. We cannot *decide* to do so, nor even anticipate such an event. Within the confines of a single project, we can do no more than follow out the logic it imposes upon us. We are not, therefore, free within the project. But nor are we free to change projects. If change there is, it comes about despite us, not because we will it.

The for-itself is therefore neither free within the project nor free to change its project. It can never choose to reject its projects, for the causes and motives of such a choice will always confirm, and never undermine, that same project. Moreover, it is easy to show that even if the for-itself could suspend its project, could confront the in-itself as it really is – assuming that it is even possible to give a sense to that phrase – it would still not be free to choose.

This must be the case, since, as we have seen, all values, all significances, come to the world through my choice. Nothing pre-exists my choice which could motivate it. Thus if somehow, *per impossible*, I was able to renounce my project, I would find myself confronted with pure, meaningless, brute in-itself. But, as Sartre has been at pains to insist, the in-itself cannot motivate any action. There are no causes or motives prior to the choice. Thus, confronted with this level of being, I have no reason to prefer any project to any other. I do not even possess the kind of resources that would allow me to outline a choice or to grasp the significance of a choice. In this thoroughly alien world, stripped of all human meaning, I too would not be properly human. In any case, even if I were able to choose – that is, to select one or another fundamental project – my choice would not be free. A free choice is one that selects among alternatives whose significance is understood; one that weighs up the options and assesses them in the light of their significance. A choice that is responsible for all significances cannot, by definition, refer to such pre-existing values. It is, therefore, arbitrary, and not free. This is a fact that Sartre himself realizes:

> The structure of the choice necessarily implies that it be a choice in the world. A choice which would be a choice *in terms of nothing*, a choice *against nothing*, would be a choice of nothing and would be annihilated as choice. (BN, p. 480)

The notion of choosing only makes sense *within* the world, for it is only in the world that there are options to weigh up, only in the world do things matter. But the supposed choice that is represented by the fundamental project is not a choice *within* the world; it is a choice *of* the world. It is only *subsequent* to this choice that there will be values and meanings. But that is equivalent to saying that it is not a choice at all. Rather than representing my free decision, it is the fundamental background against which I can deliberate. Since I have no reason to opt for one fundamental project rather than another – since reasons can only arise after I have chosen – my choice of fundamental project is arbitrary.

Sartre recognizes the arbitrariness of this choice; for him, this is the source of the anxiety that our freedom provokes. We feel anxious because we are obscurely (pre-ontologically) aware that we have no reason for persisting in our fundamental project which is external to that project. Since our choice does not and cannot derive 'from any prior reality' (BN, p. 464), it is fundamentally unjustifiable. For Sartre, our dim realization of this unjustifiability does not threaten our freedom. On the contrary, it is a salutary reminder of our ultimate and absolute responsibility. Since our choice is not justified by anything beyond itself, we, and we alone, are accountable for its existence. We are its only reason for being.

But this is incoherent. We are responsible for our choices only in so far as these choices are, or ought to have been, the product of a process of deliberation. We are responsible for weighing up the alternatives, calculating the consequences, and so on. Confronted with a choice within a world of values, we can be held accountable for how well we make it. We are not, and logically cannot be, responsible for a choice that brings it about that there are values. To the extent to which our responsibility is total – to the extent to which we are (causally) responsible, not just for the decision, but also for the reasons for and against that decision – the very notion of (moral) responsibility falls away. Given that *every* choice is, as Sartre says, equally unjustifiable, we can be neither blamed nor praised for making the choice we did.

Thus, despite Sartre's insistence to the contrary, we are not free in any meaningful sense to choose our fundamental project. If we have no reason for opting for one project, rather than another, our decision is not free, but merely arbitrary. Nor, however, are we free to reject a project once we have chosen it. An all-encompassing interpretation of the world presents us only with reasons for reaffirming it, and never reasons for denying it. Moreover, as we have seen, if we were able to reject our fundamental project, we would find ourselves facing a meaningless world. The transition from one project to another cannot be made *for reasons*, since reasons exist only within projects.

We are, therefore, forced to a surprising conclusion. Freedom exists *nowhere* in *Being and Nothingness*, neither within the project – in which we simply play out the consequences of our original choice, in which the weight of my rucksack just *is* unbearable – nor between projects. We always and only have reasons to act in accordance with our fundamental project, and can never reject it or modify it with reason – which is to say that if a modification occurs, it will happen arbitrarily, without our willing it.

As we have seen, Sartre's overriding concern in writing *Being and Nothingness* was to vindicate the fundamental freedom of the human being, against determinists of all stripes. It was for the sake of this freedom that he asserted the impotence of physical causality over human beings, that he analysed the place of nothingness within consciousness and showed how it intervened between the forces that act upon us and our actions. It was in order to demonstrate our ultimate responsibility for our choices that he developed his notion of bad faith, which turns upon the manners in which people can attempt to deny their own liberty. It was to vindicate our freedom that he proposed an ethics of authenticity, according to which any action can be ethical so long as it is performed with a clear-sighted acknowledgement that it is chosen freely. Yet we are forced to conclude that Sartre's project has failed. Far from vindicating the freedom of the for-itself, *Being and Nothingness* leaves no room for it at all. If the for-itself really is just as Sartre describes it, if it chooses the world in choosing its project, then it is at least as unfree as any determinist might wish.

What has gone wrong with Sartre's project? Why has he failed to vindicate the freedom of the for-itself? A glance back at the criticisms we advanced of Sartre's theory of freedom quickly shows us where the error lies. We saw that *within* the bounds of a project there was no room for freedom. I could, for example, continue to walk despite the weight of my rucksack, the exhaustion of my legs and the heat of the sun, but not if I remained in the world of my project. It was only by bursting beyond its limits that I could act freely. But outside the project, I have no reason to act in any particular manner at all. I leave all reasons behind when I leave the project. I am, therefore, no freer when I find myself beyond all limits than I was when I found myself constrained by them.

If I am to be really free, then, I must be able to find myself in a position midway between these two extremes. I must be able to find myself in a world that is *already* meaningful, for choice has no place in a world from which meanings and values are absent. Freedom cannot exist in a world which is pure in-itself. On the other hand, however, these meanings in which I find myself immersed, which pre-exist me and for which I am not (causally) responsible, must not so confine me, so determine my actions, that I merely act out the options they decide for me. I must find myself inhabiting an already meaningful world, if I am to be free, but I must be able to distance myself from these meanings, to evaluate them, to weigh them up. It is only on this condition, on condition that alternative courses of action have a significance that is independent of me, that things matter, whether I wish them to or not, that I have the resources available for me to decide responsibly. If I am to weigh my options, they must already have a weight. But this weight cannot be so crushing that nothing is left for me to decide.

Choice, therefore, has a place only within an already significant world. The question we must now ask ourselves is this: could Sartre acknowledge this fact while yet retaining the main lines of his thought? Does the recognition that freedom must be *situated* in order to be possible spell the end of the existentialist project? Or might it be accommodated within a reformulated existentialism?

There are, it seems to me, two manners in which the fact that freedom must be situated to be genuine might be accommodated – that is, two different ways in which we might hold that actions have a significance that precedes us and is independent of us. We might, first of all, argue that human actions have a significance that is biological. We might, for example, hold that, given the kinds of creatures we are, certain actions just are in our interests, and others against them, independently of what we think those interests are. We might revive the Aristotelian position, according to which human beings have a *telos*, a good at which they naturally aim, or a function, which they and they alone are naturally suited to perform. In its sociobiological form, something like this argument is quite frequently encountered. As we have seen, this family of positions is unified by the fact that all its members hold that human beings have a *nature*, and it is this nature which serves as the standard against which actions can be measured.

It should be obvious that this position is anathema to Sartre. If freedom can be rescued only by supposing that we have a nature, then it is clear that the existentialist project is doomed. The entire edifice is constructed around the proposition that we have no such nature; that our existence precedes our essence and therefore that it is up to humanity to decide what we are and ought to be. We cannot accept the claim that we have a nature, that there is a manner in which our biology determines us to be, and remain disciples of Sartre.

Saying this does not constitute an argument against the sociobiological position. Nevertheless, we have good reason to be suspicious of this view. For one thing, the sheer empirical diversity of human cultures constitutes a powerful reason to think that we have no truly substantive nature; that our biology places none but the broadest constraints on the ways in which human beings can live. The historical and anthropological evidence seems consistent with the Sartrean position, that though we share a human *condition*, we have no shared *nature*.

Fortunately, therefore, both for the sake of the Sartrean project and for the sake of human freedom, there is an alternative available to us which will enable us to acknowledge that significances pre-exist our choices. On this view, values and meanings come to the world not through the forces of biology, but through human culture. We are, each of us, born into a world that is already conferred with meaning, in which hodological paths have been carved out, in which certain enterprises count as meaningful and others as trivial, all independently of our choices. We find ourselves in such a world of meanings merely by being born into a particular human culture. It is cultures which confer significance on to the world, not individuals; it is cultures which constitute the background of meaning against which each of us makes our way. By establishing a world of meanings, human cultures lay down the necessary preconditions for us to weigh our options; they bring it about that things matter. They therefore open up lines that we can follow through, while closing off possibilities for us. Yet they do not *determine* our behaviour. They merely open a space in which free action is possible.

I contend that if human freedom is a coherent possibility, it will exist as free action within a world opened up and made meaningful for us, prior to our choices, and that the agent of this opening will be culture. If this is correct, then it will remain the case that our freedom is limited only by human freedom itself, for cultures have no existence apart from the actions of their members which sustain them. Thus, the fundamental postulate of existentialism – that it is up to humanity to decide what it shall be, without excuse or justification – will hold true. Yet each of us will be able to act responsibly, for though cultures exist only through our actions, and we therefore remain free to challenge every aspect of our culture, we cannot hold the entire system in abeyance. Rather, its meanings and significances will provide us with the background against which we can choose. Human freedom, considered at the level of the culture, will be absolute, but each individual will find their sphere of action limited by the very background that makes it possible. Our freedom will be concrete, precisely because it is situated: we will be free, not to do anything whatsoever, but to make something of that which is given to us.

My claim is not merely that this position is compatible with the main lines of Sartrean existentialism. I think we can go further, and argue that it is precisely towards such a position that the later Sartre moved. Though Sartre never criticized his earlier, explicitly existentialist thought along the lines I have suggested, he did recognize that *Being and Nothingness* remained too abstract to constitute an accurate and useful depiction of human life, and therefore began the process of making his philosophy more concrete. He did so by turning to Marxism. What Marxism provided Sartre with was a powerful *historical* mode of thought: a mode of thought which insisted on situating the individual in a particular history, thinking and acting with the tools which that history makes available to that individual. That is, Marxism allowed Sartre to situate the for-itself, to insist on its position in a world not of its own making and show how it was that it could act in that world, against the background of its own history. We shall follow Sartre in elaborating this thought in the second part of this book.

FURTHER READING

After being out of fashion for a long time, existential psychoanalysis is making something of a comeback, in part owing to the growth of interest in 'philosophical counselling'. The classic statement of Sartre-inspired existential psychoanalysis is perhaps R.D. Laing's *The Divided Self: An Existential Study in Sanity and Madness* (Harmondsworth: Penguin, 1965). Rollo May (ed.) *Existential Psychology*, 2nd edn (New York: McGraw-Hill, 1969) is a useful collection. On philosophical counselling in general, see Lou Marinoff, *Plato, Not Prozac!* (London: HarperCollins, 2000).

Sartre's theory of freedom has generated a large literature. The criticism I level at it in this chapter is not entirely original; Linda Bell, in *Sartre's Ethics of Authenticity* (Tuscaloosa: University of Alabama Press, 1989), sketches some of the same points (though Bell does not believe, as I do, that the flaws outlined are fatal). As early as 1955, Maurice Merleau-Ponty, Sartre's colleague at *Les Temps Modernes*, outlined much the same argument in the chapter devoted to Sartre in *Adventures of the Dialectic*, trans. Joseph Bien (Evanston, IL: Northwestern University Press, 1973). Charles Taylor levels the same criticisms at some versions of liberal philosophy in his *Ethics of Authenticity* (Cambridge, MA: Harvard University Press, 1992).

THE LATER SARTRE

In the first part of this book, we examined the major themes of Sartre's existentialism in so far as they bear on his central philosophical preoccupation: the possibility of human freedom. We laid out Sartre's arguments for the view that we each confer significance upon a world that, prior to our existence, is devoid of all meaning. Because this significance depends entirely on us, Sartre claimed that we always remain free to alter it. But, as we also saw, the very radicalness of this freedom emptied it of all content. One cannot coherently choose in a world in which the meaning of all choices must itself be chosen. True freedom can exist only in a world that is meaningful independently of our choices.

Thus Sartre's existentialist thought, for all its many insights into human conduct and self-deception, was fundamentally flawed. His account of human action does not vindicate our fundamental liberty. Instead, if it were true, it would demonstrate its impossibility.

Although he never said as much, Sartre seems to have come to perceive the failure of his existentialist project, and to have diagnosed correctly the cause of this failure. So much we can deduce from the fact that he did not long continue to elaborate his existentialism, but soon set off in a new direction. Over the fifteen years following the publication of *Being and Nothingness*, Sartre slowly felt his way towards Marxism, and in 1960 he published his second major work, a contribution towards Marxist social theory. This new work, *The Critique of Dialectical Reason*, remains concerned with the possibility of human freedom. Sartre will always maintain that such freedom remains our essential characteristic. But for the new Sartre, this freedom will be essentially situated; our choices will exist within the framework of a world imbued with meanings we do not choose. Thus our freedom will be more limited. But, just for that reason, it will be more substantial.

The second part of the book is devoted to an examination of Sartre's Marxism. This examination will be rather less detailed than the first half: Sartre's Marxism is an extraordinary contribution to social theory, but a detailed examination of its major topic, the nature of human collectives, would take us too far away from our main concerns. Thus we will touch on its central themes only in so far as they suggest ways in which we might solve our primary problem: how to vindicate the possibility of human freedom.

Existentialism and Marxism

Sartre's gradual turn toward Marxism is, in many ways, an astonishing development. On a number of fronts, existentialism is fundamentally opposed to the main themes of Marxism. Existentialism, at least in Sartre's hands, is resolutely individualistic; it contends that it is up to each of us, individually, to confer meaning upon our world, and to make our own way in it. Marxism, on the other hand, is centred around the notion of social classes; for Marx, what we are and what we are capable of doing and thinking is largely a product of our society and the position we occupy within it. Whereas the existentialist Sartre had always claimed that nothing can act on human consciousness, given its ontological status, for Marx human consciousness is a product of material forces:

> It is not the consciousness of men that determines their social being, but, on the contrary, their social being that determines their consciousness.[22]

Marx is here claiming that the circumstances of human life determine the kinds of thoughts we are capable of having. In particular, the 'mode of production' – the fundamental economic structure of a particular society, whether, for example, it is agricultural or industrial – determines our ideas. Our conception of ourselves, our society, the universe and the meaning of human history is a product of our place in this fundamental economic structure, a distorted and all too dim reflection of material reality. Since the mode of production varies from society to society, and in particular from epoch to epoch, human consciousness alters over time. Thus, Marx's thought is *historicist*: it claims that in a deep sense what we are changes throughout human history.

This view of the relation between human consciousness and the mode of production is vividly, if a little crudely, summed up in the famous Marxist image of the base and superstructure. The base, the economic foundation of society, determines the form and content of the superstructure, which contains all the elements of a society which we might refer to as its culture, from its philosophy to its legal system, from its aesthetic products to its notions of politeness.

We need go no further with this thumbnail sketch of Marx's thought to glimpse the fundamental opposition between it and Sartrean existentialism. In *Being and Nothingness* Sartre held that we each freely confer significance on a fundamentally meaningless in-itself, which is unable to act upon us in turn. Marx suggests that precisely the opposite occurs: the material basis of society shapes the contents of our consciousness, rather than drawing its own meaning from consciousness. Sartre holds that we are radically free; Marx sees us as fundamentally constrained. We are constrained in our thinking by the ideas extant in our society; in our material freedom by the mode of production and its level of productivity, and by the restrictions placed upon each of us by the social relations that are determined by the mode of production. These latter limitations are largely the limits of social classes. In contemporary society, for example, the propertyless proletariat (the working class) is much less free than the property-owning bourgeoisie (roughly, the middle class).

To grasp just how astonishing is Sartre's gradual conversion to Marxism, we need only to consider how the Sartre of *Being and Nothingness* treated Marxist thought. For him, Marxism was a paradigm of the 'spirit of seriousness', the view that attributes more reality to the world than to human agency and which holds that the values and meanings to be found in the world are simply *there*, a part of the in-itself, independently of our choosing them. For the

Sartre of this period, this view is in bad faith. It is the view of people who deny that they are responsible for the meanings they find, who hold that causality is capable of operating on human freedom:

> It is obvious that the serious man at bottom is hiding from himself the consequences of his freedom; he is in *bad faith* and his bad faith aims at presenting himself to his own eyes as a consequence; everything is a consequence for him, and there is never any beginning … Marx proposed the original dogma of the serious when he asserted the priority of object over subject. (BN, p. 580)

Thus for the existentialist Sartre, Marx was in bad faith; in maintaining that our material conditions determine our consciousness, he was guilty of asserting the priority of the material over the subjective, and thus of denying human freedom. In so doing, Marx missed the only true beginning in human affairs, which lies in the power of subjectivity to interrupt the causal chains that would act upon it and to initiate actions that are not determined by material conditions.

Given this fundamental conflict between the fundamental tenets of Marxism and those of Sartre's own thought, how did it happen that Sartre found himself edging nearer and nearer to embracing his foe? There were, I suggest, two reasons for his gradual change of heart, one philosophical, the other political.

The philosophical reason we have already glimpsed, at least in part. As it stood, Sartre's theory of human freedom was fundamentally flawed. He needed some explanation of how it was that human actions could have a significance that did not need to be chosen afresh upon each occasion, but which could pre-exist our choices, in order to give some content to the latter. There are two manners in which this hole at the centre of Sartre's thought could be filled; two ways in which he could coherently argue that our actions have a meaning and a value that exist independently of our choices. The first is by reinstating the idea of a human nature. If indeed we have such a nature, then there are facts about us – about our interests and what will serve them, about what constitutes our welfare, in what kind of society we will find fulfilment, and so on – that are simply given. If we have such a nature, then this nature can provide the fixed background against which we choose, and so impart content to Sartre's philosophy of freedom.

It should be obvious that Sartre would be extremely unwilling to take this path. The denial that there is such a thing as human nature is almost as fundamental to his thought as is the insistence upon human freedom itself. Reinstate that nature and his entire philosophy collapses. Though it may be possible to elaborate a philosophy of freedom on the foundation of a theory of human nature (so long as that nature is not pictured as too narrowly prescriptive), there would be nothing Sartrean about such a philosophy.

Fortunately for Sartre, there is another path open to him by which freedom can be given a content, another way in which it might be held that our actions have a significance that is not chosen. This significance could come to them not from our nature, but from our society. According to this line of thought, though we have no nature, in the sense of an ahistorical essence, we cannot help regarding some things as significant and others as trivial, for we have been *acculturated* to value them in this way. That is to say, we have been brought to share (most of) the values of our culture, to see the world through its eyes. Our very identity is a social product, one that we cannot reject while maintaining our grip on reality. For even our notion of what an individual is – and therefore of what we ourselves are – comes to us from our culture. We are the products of our culture through and through; it is against the background of its ideals and its values that we live out our moral lives, and we think utilizing its concepts.

Plainly, this theory will fill the gap in Sartre's philosophy of freedom. It provides him with a background of significances which, themselves unchosen, can confer content on our choices. It does so, moreover, without requiring us to suppose that there is such a thing as a timeless human essence. What we are will vary through time and according to the culture in which we find ourselves. Finally, this is a theory that is intrinsically plausible, or at least so it seems to many philosophers. It helps explain, for example, the great variety of actual variation we see in the values of different cultures. Moreover, it is a politically attractive view (for someone who shares Sartre's leftist attitudes): since it holds that what human beings are is amenable to change, it offers the political activist the hope of transforming society and humanity for the better. Under the name of 'communitarianism', it has in recent years come to be one of the major strands of political philosophy in the Anglo-American tradition, and something like it is taken for granted by a great many sociologists, anthropologists and other social scientists.

It is this historicist picture of the human being and of human meaning which Sartre was to find in Marxism. It was, after all, Marx who held that 'all history is nothing but a continuous transformation of human nature'.[23] Thus, by turning to Marx, Sartre could fill the gap in his philosophy of freedom that threatened it with incoherence, and finally formulate a defensible theory of human action.

Marxism emphasizes the importance of social classes. It is a social class – the proletariat – which is to be the agent of revolution; it is action in concert which brings about social change. But the Sartre of *Being and Nothingness*, as we saw, professed a profoundly solipsistic doctrine, according to which subjects were always and necessarily engaged in a kind of battle of wills with one another, as each attempted to objectify the other and escape objectification. It is apparent that Sartre could not subscribe to Marxist theory without abandoning this solipsism.

Fortunately, the historicist view of human meanings that is part and parcel of Marxism will allow Sartre to rethink interhuman relations. It is only because each human being, in the universe of *Being and Nothingness*, is an independent source of meaning and significance that the gaze of the other person represented such a threat to the existentialist Sartre. The other appeared to him then as a being who, in the midst of my world, could qualify it with meanings that were inaccessible to me, who could be the foundations of aspects of *my* being. Once, however, Sartre recognizes that meanings do not have their source in the look or the thoughts of other individuals, the threat they represent is dramatically reduced. No longer will he be forced to imagine that the relationships between people is necessarily reducible to a sinister play of mutual objectifications, and the way is open to him to reconceive human relationships more positively.

The view that what human beings, most essentially, are is itself subject to historical transformation is not unique to Marx. Sartre could have found it elsewhere: in Nietzsche, for example, at least on a certain reading of him (indeed, Sartre's post-structuralist critics took precisely the Nietzschean route to a similar position on human nature). But Sartre had other, more directly political reasons for embracing Marx.

Sartre had always been on the left, politically. But during the first years of his celebrity, he refrained from direct involvement in party political affairs. In the France of the 1950s, however, it seemed to him that it was necessary to take sides. The final straw, for him, was the arrest in 1952 of Jacques Duclos, one of the leaders of the French Communist Party, on charges of plotting against the security of the state (Duclos had with him two pigeons, destined for his dining table, which the police took to be a clandestine method of communicating with Moscow). Angered by the hypocrisy of the French right, Sartre threw his intellectual prestige behind the communists, though he never joined their party. He began to read Marx more sympathetically and to explore the growing body of Marxian thought in depth.

Though Sartre became a 'fellow traveller', as sympathizers with the Communist Party were called, he found the Marxist literature in which he immersed himself immensely dissatisfying. Especially in the hands of Stalinist ideologues, the subtleties of Marxist explanation had become a crude and mechanistic tool. The economic base of a society was held to govern strictly its ideological superstructure. Thus politics – indeed, all meaningful human activity – became a merely epiphenomenal activity, determined by the mode of production. On this view, history becomes a mere unfolding of the iron laws of causality, and humans, far from being its agents, became mere cogs in its mechanism.

Sartre could not accept this view, since it denies the reality of human freedom. Sartre remains Sartre, for all his new openness to Marxism. Moreover, as he was quick to point out, the view that political events are determined by the iron laws of history is, even on orthodox Marxist terms, incoherent. If history is a story driven by its own internal mechanisms, if the free choices of individual agents count for nothing, then why be a Marxist at all? If we are powerless to affect the outcome, then why struggle? A political position that claims that our actions are irrelevant to the course of history ought to be a recipe for quietism, not a call to arms. Yet Marxism obviously imagines itself just such a call. If it is to make good on this claim, if it is to be able to depict itself as a fundamentally moral doctrine, which people *ought* to espouse, then it must allow a significant place for the individual and his or her choices.

Thus it seems that Marxism needs (something like) existentialism, just as much as existentialism needs Marxism. If Sartre requires some means whereby values and significances can be held relatively constant, to form a background against which the agent can act, the Marxist needs some means whereby to think individual freedom. In good dialectical fashion, each is by itself merely abstract, offering only half-truths. Together, they offer the hope of understanding the social world and our place within it.

The structure of the *Critique of Dialectical Reason*

The result of Sartre's struggles to integrate existentialism with Marxism is the *Critique of Dialectical Reason*. A vast, sprawling book, the *Critique* was written at white heat, powered by a (then legal) mixture of aspirin and amphetamines. Sartre ruined his health in writing it, only to see it overshadowed by the tidal wave of structuralism; by the time it appeared in 1960, Sartre's star was on the wane in the French intellectual scene. Perhaps the relative lack of success of the *Critique* was inevitable; its topic – the conditions under which truly collective action is possible – is relatively esoteric, when compared with the concerns of *Being and Nothingness*, and Sartre's convoluted and difficult treatment of his theme defeats all but the most determined readers. Nevertheless, beneath the verbiage and the repetition, the *Critique* is a truly significant book. We cannot hope to do it justice here. Instead, we must rest content with a thumbnail sketch.

The *Critique* can be read as having two major, intertwined themes. The first concerns the possibility of revolution. The question that Sartre sets out to answer, under this heading, is this: under what conditions will individuals, perhaps even the fiercely independent individuals who people existentialist writings, join together in the common project of risking their lives for the sake of a new political order? To answer this question, Sartre depicts a kind of ideal-type history; he demonstrates the mechanisms whereby individuals are normally isolated from one another and from political action, and outlines the paths that might lead them from this state to the moment when they constitute an active group.

The second major theme that animates the *Critique* might be said to be a continuation of the concerns of *Being and Nothingness*. Just as in that earlier work, Sartre is here concerned with the relationship between humanity and the material world, between what he had once termed the 'for-itself' and the 'in-itself'. But whereas for the existentialist Sartre, matter was mere inanimate clay, to be given what significance we like, now Sartre grasps the full extent to which matter can constitute a real limitation on our freedom. As Sartre himself summed up the fundamental difference in outlook which distinguishes his later philosophical work from the earlier, 'life taught me *la force des choses* – the power of circumstances'.[24]

These two central themes of the *Critique* are developed together. It is *la force des choses* which constitutes the power separating individuals from each other, preventing them coming together and taking active control of their lives. More precisely, it is matter in so far as it is *worked*, as it bears the imprint of human labour, which turns against the very people whose labour it is, undermining their projects and turning each against every other.

Sartre thus begins his ideal-type history where we might expect a Marxist to begin: with labour. The world we inhabit, Sartre claims, is a world of scarce resources. There is simply not enough by way of the means of life to go round, and what there is must be wrested from the earth by means of great effort. Thus we are each forced to work for the bread that maintains us. As we labour, we transform the world: it takes on the imprint of our work. Wild nature is remade into regular fields; cities spring up, roads snake across the land. The world becomes a thoroughly human space. But not necessarily a hospitable place: the transformation of the world does not always have the consequences we desire. Matter reflects back the human activity it absorbs, it becomes a kind of quasi-agent in its own right. It becomes, to use Sartre's new terminology, 'practico-inert': completely inert, in so far as it is mere matter, yet capable of all too practical effects.

There is nothing inherently sinister about the practico-inert; in fact, it makes possible almost everything we call culture. We travel on roads that have been opened up for us by others, both literally and metaphorically, and if these past actions have closed off many avenues to us, they have opened up many others. But very often, the practico-inert has effects the very opposite of those we intend. It escapes, as it were, from the project that forms it, and reacts back against that project. Often, this occurs precisely because the action in question is that of isolated individuals. For example, in one of Sartre's most vivid illustrations of this effect, the actions of Chinese peasants over a period of four thousand years, in clearing land of trees, has reacted against those same peasants. Four thousand years of tree clearing has left China deforested. Without vegetation to hold it in place, the silt of the mountains is continually washed into the rivers by the rains, raising their water levels. Floods become more and more frequent. Thus, the human activity aimed at increasing the productivity of the land, enabling it to support more people, has resulted in terrible floods, which wash away topsoil and have been responsible for many thousands of deaths (over two thousand in 1998 alone).

This tendency of matter to channel the labour it absorbs in directions that run counter to those intended by the people whose labour it is Sartre calls 'counter-finality'. It arises most commonly as a result of the concatenation of thousands of isolated actions, each of which is innocuous taken by itself, but the combined effect of which is to worsen the position of all the actors. The effects of counter-finality are ubiquitous in social and economic life: runaway inflation, for example, is often triggered in just such a manner (as Sartre illustrates with the example of the importation of the gold of the New World to Spain in the sixteenth century).[25]

If counter-finality arises, for the most part, as a result of a lack of coordination between the actions of isolated individuals, then it seems obvious that it is circumvented by cooperation between people. The difficulty that arises here, according to Sartre, is that under conditions of scarcity, the practico-inert has the effect of enforcing isolation. In a world of scarce resources, each of us is the rival of every other. The radical individualism that was Sartre's starting point in *Being and Nothingness* is here explained not as a necessary ontological postulate, but as an imposed effect of scarcity and the practico-inert.

An illustration of the manner in which the practico-inert separates each of us from every other might help clarify Sartre's point. Sartre himself offers us the everyday example of people waiting for a bus. Each person here is unified with every other by the fact that they wait for the same bus; as a collectivity, they have their being outside of them, in the bus. But by the same token, the structure of the activity in which they are all engaged isolates them from each other. They all act under conditions of scarcity; in this case, the scarcity of seats on the bus. Each is thus forced, by the material constraints of the situation, to view the others as competitors for the same scarce resource. Because, so far as the activity of travelling by bus is concerned, each person in the queue is the same as every other, all are rivals:

> Thus the specific scarcity – the number of people in relation to the number of places – in the absence of any particular practice, would designate every individual as dispensable; the Other would be the rival of the Other because of their identity. (CDR, p. 260)

This mode of being together in isolation Sartre will call the 'series'. Each individual here exists as a member of a series.

The series is the primary manner in which people live, in all societies. Everywhere that people exist as interchangeable, so that each competes with every other for scarce resources, they exist as serialized individuals. As members of a series, each is isolated from every other, whether they act in close proximity – in the bus queue or at the stock market, for example – or whether they are physically isolated (each of us watching the same programme on television in our own lounge rooms, for example). So long as we exist in series, we are unable to coordinate our actions, and the risk that they will rebound against us is high.

Thus, if we are to become capable of directing our individual and social lives, we need to find a way to emerge from the series. We need to change the manner in which we exist together, so as to become capable of coordinating our actions. In Sartre's terminology, we need to be able to form a 'fused group'.

But we cannot change the ontological status of our collectives, from series to fused groups, simply by willing it. The practico-inert structures that surround us all conspire to maintain us in the series, and though we might each wish for a more authentic community, scarcity requires us to see every other person as an actual or potential rival. Gone is the voluntarism of *Being and Nothingness*: the conditions of exiting from the series are not psychic, but material. It is only under the right kind of circumstances that series have the possibility of forming themselves into groups. Though the fused group, and the fused group alone, is capable of snatching back the power of autonomous action and self-direction from the practico-inert world of worked matter, it is only on the basis of the right disposition of matter that the group can emerge.

What are the circumstances under which the series can become a fused group? Sartre answers this question by reference to the coming of the French Revolution. The people of Paris lived, in 1789, in series; they formed a collective only in so far as they were unified by the practico-inert outside of them. This remained the case, even as the political temperature rose, and the King faced the revolt of the third estate. It was only when the rumours began to fly that the troops surrounding Paris were there to besiege, perhaps even attack, the city that people's consciousness of themselves and of each other changed. Now each saw in every other no longer the competitor for scarce resources of the series, but instead the potential victim of the troops' repression. In face of the common danger, each sees the other as himself or herself. Hence, by sending troops to surround the city, '[t]he government constituted Paris as a totality from outside' (CDR, p. 352).

Thus the series begins to collapse in the face of imminent danger. Group solidarity increases in proportion to the peril. As yet, the risk is still rather abstract; though people feel themselves at risk and look with new eyes at their neighbours as potential allies, it is not until the danger is imminent that the group, as an active agent, forms. Once again, the circumstances under which this occurs are material. The people of the Sainte-Antoine district lived in the shadow of the Bastille. Thus, their practico-inert field was structured in an especially threatening manner. For them, the danger was imminent: they were within range of the fortress's cannons. Moreover, the possibility existed for them that if the troops surrounding Paris entered the city to put down rebellion, these people would find themselves caught between the Bastille and the troops: unable to flee, too lightly armed to defend themselves, they would be massacred.

For the population of this district, then, the menace was ever-present, the stakes life itself. Under the pressure of circumstances – *la force des choses* – the group is born from the ashes of the series; since the practico-inert field is structured so that action is demanded, the group is active. On 14 July 1789, the mob stormed the Bastille. The people of Paris had transformed themselves from passive quasi-objects into active subjects; they were making their own history.

But Sartre's ideal-type history is circular; he traces the transformation of the series into the group, and back again. The group gradually loses its active character and eventually collapses back into the series. Indeed, this decomposition seems inevitable: if the group is formed only under extreme pressure, then it must decay as the danger to which it is a reaction passes. Sartre traces the process whereby the group is transformed from a spontaneous, almost organic entity into an institution. A great many insights are to be gleaned here about the manner in which revolutionary movements often come to resemble the regimes they aimed to overthrow. Examining this apparently inevitable corrosion would, however, take us too far afield. It is time to return to our central theme. How do Sartre's insights into the manner in which collectives transform themselves from passive quasi-objects into active subjects bear on our examination of the conditions under which freedom is possible? We shall address this question in the next, and final, chapter.

FURTHER READING

In developing a version of Marxism which is oriented more towards social than economic analysis, Sartre was participating in a larger movement, which has come to be known as 'Western Marxism' (in order to distinguish it from the cruder version that was the official ideology of the Soviet Union). On this topic, Perry Anderson's *Considerations on Western Marxism* (London: NLB, 1976) is a classic, and Ben Agger's *Western Marxism: An Introduction: Classical And Contemporary Sources* (Santa Monica: Goodyear, 1979) also deserves a mention. Mark Poster's *Existential Marxism in Postwar France: From Sartre to Althusser* (Princeton: Princeton University Press, 1975) places Sartre's turn to Marxism in context illuminatingly, and the same author's *Sartre's Marxism* (London: Pluto Press, 1979) is the best short exposition of the *Critique* in print.

Norman Geras's *Marx and Human Nature: Refutation of a Legend* (London: Verso, 1983) convincingly states the case for the view that Marx did subscribe to a notion of a substantive human nature.

Many books have been written on the prisoner's dilemma. I find Frederic Schick's *Making Choices: A Recasting of Decision Theory* (New York: Cambridge University Press, 1997) one of the clearest on the topic.

Sartre's second philosophy of freedom

It should be obvious that in discussing the birth of the group from the ashes of the series, Sartre is directly concerned with the possibility of human freedom. In so far as we belong to a series, we are powerless to take charge of our own lives. As we have already seen, the isolated individual of the series is constantly prey to counter-finality; unable to coordinate her actions with those of others, she constantly witnesses them rebound against her. In so far as we exist in series, moreover, we are vulnerable to what Sartre calls 'other-direction', in which the series is manipulated by people who take its members as objects (whether for the purpose of selling them soap powder or of keeping the working class docile).

Thus the series is the milieu of impotence. Recall how, in *Being and Nothingness*, Sartre had denied that human beings were ever the objects of causal processes. The Marxist Sartre would not so much retract as modify this contention: now his claim is that it is only in so far as we belong to a series that we are subject to causal laws. The so-called 'laws' of economics, for example, are real enough; however, they are laws that apply only to the series. Indeed, the actions of individuals competing with one another in the marketplace (just like the actions of the participants in the prisoner's dilemma) are rather predictable. But this is not because human beings are always and necessarily subject to these laws. It is only in so far as we are isolated that we are unfree.

Accordingly, it is only in so far as we exit from the series that we begin to act in concert, and only when we are not in competition with each other that we can begin to be free. The fused group snatches the possibility of freedom from serialized impotence. The series channels the actions of the people who constitute it into the practico-inert, whence it rebounds against them; the group is formed as the project of mastering the practico-inert, and thus returning to its members power over their own labour. The group

> produces itself through the project of taking the inhuman power of mediation between men away from worked matter and giving it, in the community, to each and to all and constituting itself … as a resumption of control over the materiality of the practical field. (CDR, p. 672)

For all the transformations his thought has undergone, Sartre's remains a philosophy of freedom. His first and constant concern is with the possibility of each of us directing our own lives as we would wish.

But is this new approach to human action any less flawed than the first? We saw the philosophy of freedom of the existentialist Sartre collapse into incoherence because of its failure to take sufficient account of the material conditions under which freedom must be exercised. Action that occurs against a void, which decides the meaning of the background against which it acts, at the same time as it chooses how to react to that background is not free; it is merely arbitrary. The *Critique of Dialectical Reason* seems to fill this gaping hole in Sartre's thought: by emphasizing the material background against which we act and explaining how that background enters into and conditions the action, Sartre provides himself with the missing ingredient in his theory of freedom.

But in doing so, he runs a great risk. If it is true that there must be a relatively fixed background against which we act, if our actions are to be free, by the same token too great a rigidity in this background is as certain to destroy freedom as is too little. If it is true that without values and significances independent of us, to which we can refer in making our choices, our actions are merely arbitrary, the fact remains that if these same values and significances are fixed beyond appeal or transformation, then our actions will be determined by them.

Thus, if he has over-emphasized the material background against which we choose, Sartre will have as surely evacuated freedom from the world of the *Critique* as he had from *Being and Nothingness*. If, for example, the fused group that stormed the Bastille was determined from outside, by the danger in which the people of Paris found themselves, then the action in which they subsequently engaged was not free. In that case, it was *caused* by the material circumstances. It no more deserves the epithet 'free' than does the behaviour of litmus paper dipped in an acid.

Sartre is well aware of this danger, and careful to avoid it. It is precisely this trap which he criticizes conventional Marxists for falling into when they hold that revolution is inevitable and the laws of history are inexorable. Such laws do not, Sartre insists, apply to human beings in so far as they are free, that is, in so far as they exist as members of a fused group. Since it is the fused group, and not the series, which takes history into its hands and makes the revolution, there cannot be any such inexorable laws having revolution as their outcome. Moreover, if there were, Marxism would be incoherent. It would be drained of its moral charge: rather than being the doctrine that represents the best hope for humanity, it would be no more than the value-free observation of the regularities of history.

As we can now see, a coherent philosophy of freedom involves a difficult balancing act. It must acknowledge the role of material factors, and of significances that exist independently of historical actors, lest it fall into the pitfalls that ultimately undermined the existentialist doctrine. On the other hand, it must not allow these material factors too large a place, lest it replace freedom of action with the determinism of objective forces. How, then, does Sartre propose to balance these two opposing forces in his philosophy of freedom?

In the first place, Sartre continues to argue that freedom remains irreducible to objective factors. Certainly, it is true that it is only under particular historical circumstances that the fused group can form. The Bastille could not have been stormed if the troops had not encircled Paris, or if the population of the Sainte-Antoine district had felt themselves to have an accessible escape route. But this does not imply that we can formulate a historical law that would capture the actions of the Paris mob; a law holding, for example, that

> Whenever the population of a region feels itself to be in mortal peril, without possibility of escape, it will throw off the shackles of seriality and become a fused group.

Since the fused group is a product, as well as the occasion, of free action, there cannot be any such law in principle. And a little empirical study will show that there is no such law. It simply isn't the case that fused groups always form in the circumstances envisaged. Though the group arises only in the appropriate circumstances, it does not arise *whenever* circumstances are propitious. Action, freely engaged in, remains irreducibly necessary.

Does this imply that freedom remains fundamentally mysterious, a magical power that – inexplicably – might or might not appear whenever the material circumstances are appropriate? Not at all. Sartre is insistent that though it is only when we enter into the fused group that we are fully free, in the sense that we become fully capable of directing our lives, nevertheless freedom is never absent from human action. The action – Sartre calls it 'praxis', utilizing a word beloved of Marxists – that rebounds against the serialized individual remains free. It is only because the Chinese peasants freely chose to chop down trees that they became the victims of counter-finality. Freedom is always and everywhere present in human affairs, though the ability to take charge of one's destiny requires the birth of the fused group from the ashes of the series.

What, then, is the precise relation between freedom and materiality? Let us consider an example from the *Critique*, in order to try to answer this question.

The example is banal enough. It concerns the practice among sceptical, or even atheist, Catholics of nevertheless baptizing their children. As Sartre shows, though the example seems trivial, it has the question of freedom at its heart. These Catholic parents baptize their children in the belief that so doing will maximize their freedom: it will leave the decision whether or not to remain in the church up to the children, when they come of age (some Jews circumcize their sons for similar reasons).

But is it true that by baptizing their children, these parents open up more options for them than otherwise? Sartre argues that it is not. The lapsed Catholic baptizes their child as a way of *postponing* the decision whether the child is to belong to the church. But the decision cannot be postponed; it must be taken now and attempting to postpone it is merely one way in which it can be taken. 'Whatever one does, in fact, one *prejudges*':

> it is necessary to decide the meaning of faith (that is to say, of the history of the world, of mankind) on behalf of the child, and without being able to consult him ... whatever one does, and whatever precautions one takes, he will bear the weight of this decision throughout his life. (CDR, p. 486 note 45).

By baptizing him, one is not postponing the decision concerning religion until the child is of age. One is instead making it for him, as surely as if one decided against baptism. Of course, the precise meaning of one's act is not yet settled. It must be made concrete, in the manner in which the child is brought up. Do the parents send him to a religious school and insist he attend mass regularly, all in the name of putting off the decision a little longer? If so, then they decide on a Catholic childhood for him; they make it the case that whatever he does in his adult life, he will be irredeemably marked, for himself as well as for others, as having been Catholic. They also make it far more likely that he will remain in the church than if they sent him to a secular school, or communicated their sceptical doubts to him. Of course, it is not the case that by sending him to the latter kind of school they thereby postpone the decision. Instead, they decide that he will have a secular childhood, and thereby decrease the chances that he will be religious later in life.

The important point, from our point of view, is that here we see Sartre insisting on the importance of the material circumstances of life in the formation of the individual. The Sartre of *Being and*

Nothingness would have held that the child brought up as a Catholic had a Catholic past but that, since we are each a continual wrenching of ourselves away from our past, he would *now* have a clean slate; he would remain Catholic only by freely reaffirming the choice of Catholicism. Now, however, Sartre recognizes that the manner in which we have been brought up – not just the religion we have been taught, but the values inculcated in us and those we have absorbed, the cultural meanings that surround us and make us the kinds of people we are – forms the horizon within which we think and act. It is only against the background of this past, these meanings and values, that we choose. It is they which confer a significance upon our choices and rescue them from being arbitrary. It is they which give a *content* to freedom.

But if it is freedom that is in question here, and not the manner in which circumstances – upbringing, culture and so on – *determine* action, then it cannot be the case that we must simply act in accordance with these meanings and values. The baptized child, for example, though irredeemably marked by his parents' decision, is not thereby *caused* to remain a Catholic. Though it is *this* past which he must interiorize and transcend, whether by affirming it or by rejecting it, it is only through his free project of living his life that it marks him. Immediately after the passage quoted above, Sartre adds,

> But it is also true to say that it can mark him only to the extent that he has freely interiorized it and that it becomes the free self-limitation of his freedom rather than an inert limit assigned to him by his father.

Meanings, values, the past; these are neither mechanical forces that determine our actions, nor even rigid boundaries within which we act. They are, instead, the essential background against which we always and necessarily choose. They situate our freedom, they do not destroy it. Far from it being the case, as the early Sartre seemed to think, that allowing these to mark the subject would eliminate the subject's freedom, instead they are the indispensable condition for this freedom to be concrete.

Thus the child in our example will make something of what his parents have made him. He will transcend the meaning of his childhood, as Sartre would say, when he takes it as the background against which he chooses. This will be the case no matter what he chooses: no less so if he decides to remain a Catholic than if he rejects his parents' religion.

This relatively trivial example captures, in miniature, the essence of Sartre's new philosophy of freedom. If we could express it in a formula, it might be this:

> People choose against the indispensable background of values and meanings that are independent of them. But these values and meanings form the horizon of our choices only to the extent to which we freely interiorize them by transcending them in a free action.

It might be added here that though many Marxists have seen in the *Critique* more an existentialist heresy than authentic Marxism, there is ample warrant for this view in Marx himself. It might, for instance, be read as cashing out one of Marx's most famous pronouncements about the relation between freedom and necessity in human history:

> Men make their own history, but they do not make it just as they please; they do not make it under circumstances chosen by themselves, but under circumstances directly encountered, given, and transmitted from the past.[26]

Sartre's insistence both on the material conditioning of human *praxis* and on the fact that nevertheless action can never be simply reduced to its material antecedents can productively be read as one of the most cogent attempts to explicate Marx's dictum; insisting both on the fact that it is humanity which makes history, and yet emphasizing the circumstances in which we act.

Indeed, we have yet to glimpse the full extent to which Sartre will emphasize both poles of human freedom: both its material and ideological determinants and yet its irreducible freedom. Thus far, we have examined the manner in which the past – my upbringing, my culture, and so on – enters into my free decision. We can now go further and show that the *future* plays a similar role to the past.

This would appear, at first sight, to be a nonsensical statement.

How can the future, which by definition does not yet exist, play a role in determining my decision? Since it does not exist, it cannot exert any pressure upon me; it cannot even form the background to my choices.

Nevertheless, Sartre insists upon the importance of the future in shaping human freedom. For him, the future is far from being simply non-existent. It has its own manner of being. It exists, not as something already decided, but as a network of *possibilities*. Thus, 'we must not think of it as a zone of indetermination, but rather as a strongly structured region' (SFM, p. 93). We are each born to certain future possibilities, and not to others: a child born in an industrialized country, for example, has the possibility of being a worker or a member of the bourgeoisie, but not of being a peasant. Moreover, we can go much further and assign relatively definite probabilities to whether she will be bourgeois, and, if so, just what role she will play in that class. Thus the future is already with us, already impacting on our actions and our decisions. When it comes to how this child should be educated, it will be in the light of her future possibilities that we will decide, though it is also true that our decision will help realize one possibility from this field of possibilities. In the same way, human societies as wholes have already structured fields of possibilities: destruction by nuclear holocaust is one of our possibilities, for example, a possibility that was not open to ancient Rome.

Thus human action, no matter how unexpected – and no matter whether it is the action of a serialized individual or of a fused group – does not somehow burst beyond the bounds of the present that conditions it, into a new, uncharted region. Freedom can no more create the future *ex nihilo* than it can act without reference to the given. Our actions merely bring about one from among the possibilities that are ours. This is true at both the individual and the social level (and the one by way of the other).

This is not, however, to suggest that the double conditioning of human action, by the past and by the future, means that we ought to place the emphasis on the material and ideological conditioning of action, and not on its freedom. Sartre continues the difficult balancing act, refusing to give either priority. If free action merely realizes one of the possibilities in a structured field, nevertheless it remains the case that that field itself is maintained in being only by the freedom of the acting subject. It is not as though certain possibilities will be realized, regardless of what we do, or that freedom intervenes only to divert the otherwise inevitable course of history. Whatever is brought about occurs only by way of free action. Freedom is conditioned by materiality, but materiality is the product of freedom.

Perhaps an analogy from a slightly different field, and a different philosophical tradition, would be illuminating here. The Swiss linguist Ferdinand de Saussure argued that in thinking about language we ought to distinguish two elements. The first element, which he called *langue*, refers to language as a *system* of signs. *Langue* is an abstract entity, which is to be opposed to language in use, which Saussure calls *parole*. Every single act of communication in language is an act of *parole*. The important thing for Saussure is that *parole* is possible only on the basis of *langue*: it is only because I have a grasp of the grammar of my language, the meaning of the lexical units that constitute it, and so on that I am able to write this sentence. Similarly, it is only because of your grasp of *langue* that you can understand the sentence. Thus, though *langue* is an abstract entity, it is an essential component of language.

Some philosophers – namely, the French structuralists, heavily influenced by Saussure – extrapolated from the claim that we think and speak only on the basis of a structured system to the conclusion that we do no more than express the possibilities of our language when we speak. We have the illusion that we use language, whereas in actuality we are its instrument. This view is expressed succinctly by Michel Foucault, for whom it is 'the structures, the system of language – and not the subject – which speaks'.[27]

This structuralist claim is closely analogous to the position of those Marxists who hold that human action is determined by its material and ideological conditioning. It is the view of those who place the emphasis exclusively on the practico-inert conditions of action and miss the essential contribution made by human freedom. In the case in hand, it misses the role of *parole* in language. Though we speak only against the background of *langue*, nevertheless *langue* itself exists only because it is constantly renewed by acts of *parole*. Language does not exist apart from its use in communication. The proof that *langue* is sustained by *parole*, if one were needed, is that language changes over time. Though we renew the system through our communicative acts, we do not replicate it exactly. Instead, it is always in flux, always changing. Nothing in the system itself can account for this change, nothing other than human freedom itself. Though we can speak only against the background it supplies, this background exists only because we speak. There is here a circle, in which neither element ought to be given priority.

Sartre is upholding a precisely analogous view, arguing that human action is possible only against the background of material and ideological conditioning, but that it is itself responsible for the existence of this very conditioning. As Marx says, we make history, but not in circumstances of our own choosing. Or as Sartre expresses it, in one of his few explicit replies to the structuralist critique of his work, '[w]hat is essential is not that man is made ... but *that he makes that which makes him*'.[28]

Thus, though our actions are always shaped and guided by the material and ideological circumstances in which we find ourselves, nevertheless we are always free. But we are not always just as free, no matter what. Sartre no longer believes, as he did in *Being and Nothingness*, that freedom is never limited by circumstances. We are always free, and always determined, but the extent to which one or other plays the greater role varies. When we exist as serialized individuals, we are more determined than we are free; though the practico-inert that steals our *praxis* from us is created by free action, we are unable to take charge of its effects. We are, instead, the victim of supposedly inexorable laws, or of the unpredictable counter-finality of matter. But when we exist in the fused group, we consciously create the conditions that determine our actions. We remain, in the vocabulary of the *Critique*, the product of our own product (SFM, p. 87); nevertheless we are engaged in the concrete project of freedom. We do not thereby break free from the field of the practico-inert; it remains the case that we merely realize one possibility from the structured field of possibilities of our society. But this does not detract from the reality of our freedom; indeed, it gives it a content. As Sartre puts it, 'what is important is not what people make of us but what we ourselves make of what they have made of us'.[29]

Though the details of this picture of freedom remain to be examined, and much remains with which we might quibble, this view of human action presents us with what I believe to be a truly coherent philosophy of freedom. It is worth pausing to examine its strengths, and to explicate the manner in which it solves the problems associated with other views. We saw how Sartre's existentialist theory failed; how it was unable to differentiate between truly free decisions and absolutely arbitrary actions. We saw that if he was to plug this gap in his thought Sartre needed to account for the manner in which choices are made against a material and ideological background – that is, against the backdrop of the meanings, values, institutions and so forth of a culture. By embracing Marxism, with its emphasis on materiality and on ideology, Sartre was able to provide this missing background.

But, as we also saw, though Sartre needed to recognize the importance of this background, this move carries with it risks. If we over-emphasize the place of the material and ideological conditionings of human action, we abolish freedom as surely as if we accorded it no place at all. We risk, that is, substituting determination by the material for the arbitrary decisions of the will.

But Sartre is never at risk of falling into this particular trap. He has learned the lessons of existentialism too well ever to deny the irreducible place of freedom in human affairs, from the most banal decisions of everyday individual life to the events that shape our history. He engages in an exquisite balancing act, refusing to give ontological priority either to the conditions of freedom or to freedom itself. Just as the Saussurian theory leads us to envisage a circle, going from the systematic features of language to speech acts and back again, so the Sartrean philosophy ought to lead us to picture a circle that leads from social structure to individual and collective action and back again. Or, changing back once more to an existentialist vocabulary, we might say that we now see that bad faith lies on both sides of human action – it does not consist just in the denial of freedom, but also in the assertion of its absoluteness.

Finally, however, if the Sartrean view is to be truly *political* – if it is to be able to guide us in our choices, to be able to differentiate which proposals and policies are progressive and which regressive – it must be the case that it gives us the means of distinguishing between circumstances and societies that are more and less free. We must be able to circumscribe regions of unfreedom in our world and imagine how they can be reduced – how the amount of freedom can be increased. A view that asserts the equi-priority of the conditionings of freedom and freedom itself is not enough if it does not allow the possibility that freedom can be reduced or increased. With his central distinction between the series and the fused group, Sartre avoids this final trap. He thereby provides us with a means of distinguishing more and less free social formations.

Thus, Sartre's philosophy fulfils all the major requirements of a theory of freedom. His journey from existentialism to Marxism was full of false starts, dead ends and failed theories, but in retrospect it can be seen as a necessary journey, one that provided him with the materials he needed to formulate a truly coherent philosophy. Sartre himself is a perfect illustration of his mature theory: we see the manner in which his thought was shaped by his ideological and material circumstances, but also the way in which he was able to transcend these circumstances, transforming himself from the product of his product into his own product. At the end of this circuitous path, Sartre has produced perhaps the most coherent picture of the relation between freedom and the social in twentieth-century thought.

Notes

1. Michel Foucault, 'L'Homme est-il mort?', *Arts et loisirs*, 15 June 1966. Cited in Didier Eribon, *Michel Foucault*, trans. Betsy Wing (Cambridge, MA: Harvard University Press, 1991), p. 161.

2. Denis Hollier, *The Politics of Prose: Essay on Sartre*, trans. J. Mehlman (Minneapolis: University of Minnesota Press, 1986), p. 92.

3. So his interviewer quotes him as describing himself, in Sartre, 'Self-Portrait at Seventy', *Life/Situations*, trans. P. Auster and L. Davis (New York: Pantheon, 1977), p. 22.

4. Paris: Editions Grasset, 2000.

5. Sartre, 'Intentionality: A Fundamental Idea of Husserl's Phenomenology', trans. Joseph P. Fell, *Journal of the British Society for Phenomenology*, 1(2) 1970, pp. 4–5.

6. Ibid., p. 5.

7. It was the desire to avoid the Cartesian – that is, dualistic – overtones of terms such as 'subject', 'human being', 'consciousness', and so on which led both Heidegger and Sartre to describe human beings using new terminology. Heidegger describes the entity usually described as a person using the everyday German word *Dasein*, in part because it captures our being-in-the-world. *Dasein* has its being (*Sein*) out there (*da*) in the world. Sartre's choice of terminology, *le pour-soi* (the 'for-itself'), instead emphasizes our ability to reflect upon ourselves (indeed, our inability *not* to do so, at least non-thetically; that is, without explicitly taking ourselves as a theme for reflection).

8. Sartre, *Nausea*, trans. Robert Baldick (London: Penguin, 1965), p. 183.

9. Ibid., p. 184.

10. Sartre, *No Exit and Three Other Plays*, trans. S. Gilbert and L. Abel (New York: Vintage, 1955), p. 47; translation slightly modified.

11. It therefore seems as though Sartre will be forced to deny the existence (or at least the effective power) of the unconscious, whether in its Freudian guise or some other. Indeed, he devotes some dense passages of *Being and Nothingness* to an attempt at a refutation of Freud. Briefly, Sartre's argument is this: According to Freud, as psychoanalysis reaches the heart of the patient's neurosis, the patient begins to resist the interpretation. Now, Sartre asks, how is this resistance possible? The resistance cannot come from the patient's ego, since the ego – which corresponds, roughly speaking, to the patient's consciousness – is on the side of the analyst. The patient has, after all, sought out treatment. Nor, however, can the resistance come from the id – which corresponds to the unconscious – since Freud supposes that the id seeks to make its desires conscious. Resistance must, therefore, come from the superego, the gatekeeper between id and ego, which examines desires and thoughts for their permissibility. The superego, however, must *know* what it is repressing – for how else would it identify the impermissible desires? It must, therefore, have knowledge that is unconscious, a 'knowledge that is ignorant of itself' (BN, p. 53), which Sartre holds to be incoherent. We shall return to this question later, with regard to the question of self-deception.

12. 'Liberalism' means many different things, but all conceptions of it share the belief that individuals are the basic political subjects, that institutions and practices are legitimate to the degree they protect or enhance individual liberty and that individuals have rights that no society may abridge. Central to all these theses is the idea that individuals are naturally – we might say ontologically – free to question their inherited values, and to that extent the Sartrean doctrine is classically liberal.

13. By making this assumption, I ignore the question whether the project itself is coherent. Some philosophers hold that we are constituted by our values and commitments, in such a manner that we cannot coherently step outside them.

14. Actually, the example Sartre depicts concerns precisely the opposite case: someone denying that he is to be identified with his sexuality. We will examine in just what senses we legitimately identify ourselves in such a manner a little later; for now I alter Sartre's example somewhat in order to make his position clear.

15. Currently, spurred in part by the recent completion of the map of the human genome, there is much debate over the influence of our genetics upon our behaviour, including our sexual behaviour. Debate has been

especially heated over the possibility that homosexuality might have a genetic basis. Many opponents of the theory that it has such a basis argue instead that it is a result of a certain kind of environment and upbringing. Sartre would deny both theories. For him, homosexuality cannot be caused by either genetics or environment, nature or nurture. It cannot be so caused because the for-itself is separated from all such causal forces by the nothingness it secretes. But if homosexuality cannot be caused by either nature or nurture, neither can heterosexuality. By nature, we are neither homosexual nor heterosexual (nor bisexual). Our sexuality is not in our nature, but up to us to invent.

16. At this point, a few words about Sartre's general attitude towards homosexuality are in order. There is no doubt that the Sartre of the 1940s and 1950s regarded homosexuality as a disorder, a kind of neurosis, as is here indicated by his use of the word 'faults'. This attitude underwent a slow transformation. In 1952, Sartre published a long, semi-biographical study of Jean Genet, an openly gay French playwright. Though *Saint Genet* contains some unfortunate 'explanations' of Genet's homosexuality in terms of his consecration of 'the priority of the object over the subject' (*Saint Genet: Actor and Martyr*, trans. B. Fretchman [London: Heinemann, 1988], p. 6), nevertheless Sartre has already advanced far enough down the road of acceptance of homosexuality for Genet to emerge from the book as a kind of paradigm of authentic humanity. By the 1970s, Sartre's attitude had transformed completely and he no longer regarded homosexuality as a deviation from a supposed norm. It is worth making two comments about this slow evolution. First, we ought to recognize that Sartre's initially derogatory attitude towards homosexuality has no warrant in his philosophy. Sartre's own professed views ought to bar him from asserting that any mode of sexual behaviour has normative status for human beings. Thus we can say of Sartre's homophobia what the contemporary French philosopher Michèle Le Dœuff says of Sartre's sexism (a sexism that underwent exactly the same evolution as his attitude towards homosexuality): that he was sexist '[a]gainst all the general assumptions of his own doctrine' (Le Dœuff, *Hipparchia's Choice: An Essay Concerning Women, Philosophy, etc.*, trans. T. Selous [Oxford: Basil Blackwell, 1991], p 68). The second point I wish to make is that, though we need to be careful when dealing with examples such as this one, nevertheless the general points Sartre makes here remain valid. If Sartre's philosophy of human existence is sound, then what he says here about homosexuality is true – and true of heterosexuality as well.

17. Sartre claims that the oscillation between my transcendence and my facticity is only one of the 'instruments of bad faith'. To it he adds the

duplicity that plays my being-for-myself off against my being-for-others (p. 57), and another that plays on temporal ambiguities (playing off my past against my always open freedom). I suspect, however, that these latter two kinds of bad faith are reducible to that which plays facticity off against transcendence. My being-for-others – the manner in which I appear to others – and my past are both aspects of my facticity. Essence is what has been, and also what is seen.

18. Sometimes the chain of reason giving will be quite long. For instance – to take another Sartrean example – when my alarm clock rings in the morning, it is 'I who confer on [it] its exigency – I and I alone' (BN, p. 38). Far from it being the case that I *must* get up when the alarm rings, that it represents an objective force that necessitates my action, I confer on it whatever power I think it has over me. But here the chain of causes that leads back to my freedom is relatively long. Perhaps the chain might go something like this: I must get up when the alarm rings because if I do not I will be late for work; if I am late for work, I will lose my job; if I lose my job, I will not be able to feed myself. But with regard to this last proposition, it is always possible to ask *why* I want to feed myself. When I ask this question, I grasp in anguish that nothing necessitates this desire of mine. Once again, my wish to preserve my life and health hangs from nothing more secure than my free choice.

19. Perhaps it would be better to say that the liar must *believe* he knows the truth. I think that we ought to say that someone is a liar if they intend to mislead, whether or not they succeed. Imagine the following scenario: I tell you that you do not need to rush to catch the next train, that it's not due for half an hour. In fact, I intend to mislead you; I have consulted the timetable and seen that the next train is due in five minutes (perhaps I have some reason to want you to miss the train). Now, it turns out that the timetable I have consulted is out of date. The next train is not due for half an hour. We will still want to say, I think, that I lied to you, even though my statement happened – accidentally – to be true. In any case, Sartre is clearly right that in paradigm cases the liar must know the truth in order to lie.

20. Sartre himself does not risk this confusion, because he does not employ the word 'cause' for either of the two factors we have identified. Instead, he distinguishes between *motifs*, which refers to the external causes of an action, and *mobiles*, which refers to subjective states. Since there is no easy way to render this distinction in English, Sartre's translator has opted to render *motif* as 'cause', reserving the term 'motive' for the internal states that motivate actions.

21. Sartre, *War Diaries: Notebooks from a Phoney War*, trans. Quintin Hoare (London: Verso, 1984), pp. 29–30.

22. Marx, 'A Contribution to the Critique of Political Economy', in *Marx and Engels: Basic Writings on Politics and Philosophy*, ed. Lewis F. Feuer (Collins, 1972), p. 84.

23. Marx, *The Poverty of Philosophy* (New York: International Publishers, n.d.), p. 124. Whether Marx himself believed in a more substantive conception of human nature is controversial, and there is a large literature on the topic. It is not necessary for us to enter into this debate. We need only to appreciate that Sartre, with some justification, read Marx as holding that if there is such a thing as human nature, it is so 'thin' and abstract as to allow for almost unlimited historical variation.

24. Sartre, 'The Itinerary of a Thought', in *Between Existentialism and Marxism*, trans. John Mathews (New York: Pantheon, 1974), p. 33.

25. The mechanisms of counter-finality have a close relative in the 'prisoner's dilemma' which analytic philosophers have explored in depth. The classic prisoner's dilemma arises when two people suspected of having committed a crime together are interviewed separately, and each is offered the following alternatives: if they confess to the crime, and their partner does not, they will be released and their uncooperative partner will get ten years' gaol. If they both confess, they will each get five years' gaol. If both are silent, there will not be enough evidence to convict either; they will instead be charged with a lesser offence and will each get one year in prison. The fascinating thing about the prisoner's dilemma is that the result of the choices of rational individuals will always be worse than might have been achieved for both, taken individually and collectively, if they had acted at random. Each individual will quickly realize that they are better off confessing, no matter what the other does (if I confess, and my partner remains silent, I will go free, but if my partner confesses I cut my sentence in half by confessing myself). Thus both suspects will confess, and both will receive five-year sentences. Yet if neither had confessed, they would each have spent only one year in prison.

Sartre's examples of counter-finality are easily analysed as variants of the prisoner's dilemma. In both cases, what appear to be individually rational actions rebound to the disadvantage of the actors. Both kinds of problem seem to be resolvable by cooperation between the parties, but just as it is notoriously difficult to make the agents in a prisoner's dilemma honour agreements, so it is difficult for Sartre's subjects to overcome the hostility that is both a cause and the product of counter-finality.

26. Marx, 'The Eighteenth Brumaire of Louis Bonaparte', in Feuer, op. cit., p. 360.

27. Foucault, 'Entretien', *La Quinzaine Littéraire*, 16 May 1966, p. 14. My translation.

28. Sartre, 'Replies to Structuralism: An Interview', trans. R. D'Amico, *Telos*, Fall 1971, p. 15.

29. Sartre, *Saint Genet*, p. 49.

Index

Note: some sub-sections are listed in page order to aid coherence; locators in brackets refer to notes.